OCS Study
MMS 2001-062

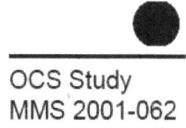

Coastal Marine Institute

Management of the MMS-LSU Coastal Marine Institute: A Report of the First Six Years, 1992-1998

I0439161

Final Report

Louisiana

Gulf of Mexico

U.S. Department of the Interior
Minerals Management Service
Gulf of Mexico OCS Region

Cooperative Agreement
Coastal Marine Institute
Louisiana State University

OCS Study
MMS 2001-062

Coastal Marine Institute

Management of the MMS-LSU Coastal Marine Institute: A Report of the First Six Years, 1992-1998

Final Report

Compiler

Robert S. Carney

August 2001

Prepared under MMS Contract
14-35-0001-30660-19918
by
Coastal Studies Institute
Louisiana State University
Baton Rouge, Louisiana 70801

Published by

U.S. Department of the Interior
Minerals Management Service
Gulf of Mexico OCS Region

Cooperative Agreement
Coastal Marine Institute
Louisiana State University

DISCLAIMER

REPORT AVAILABILITY

Extra copies of the report may be obtained from the Public Information Office (Mail Stop 5043) at the following address:

U.S. Department of the Interior
Minerals Management Service
Gulf of Mexico OCS Region
Public Information Office (MS 5034)
1201 Elmwood Park Boulevard
New Orleans, Louisiana

Telephone Number: 1-800-200-GULF or (504) 736-2519

CITATION

Suggested Citation:

Carney, R.S. 2001. Management of the MMS-LSU Coastal Marine Institute: A report of the first six years, 1992-1998; Final report. OCS Study MMS 2001-062. U.S. Dept. of the Interior, Minerals Mgmt. Service, Gulf of Mexico OCS Region, New Orleans, La. pp.

PREFACE

This is a final report of the first six years (1992-1998) of the Coastal Marine Institute (CMI) program established as a jointly funded program between Minerals Management Service (MMS) and Louisiana State University (LSU). The report is intended to review the history of the program, its objectives, and the range of studies undertaken. Each of the individual tasks either have or will submit separate final technical reports. This overview document is not intended as a duplication of that effort. Rather, it considers the general effectiveness of the CMI program.

SUMMARY

The Coastal Marine Institute (CMI) at Louisiana State University was established for an initial six years (1992-1998) as a cooperative agreement between the State and the Minerals Management Service of the U.S. Department of the Interior. The basic intent of CMI was to direct the considerable research talents of a major research university towards Federal and State information needs in a State where Outer Continental Shelf development of the oil and gas industry is a major factor. Funding for all projects undertaken has been equally divided between MMS and Louisiana resources.

During its initial six years, CMI has been exceptionally effective. Fifty projects have been funded employing the talents of 64 faculty researchers, 14 postdoctoral associates, 26 Ph.D. candidates, 22 master's candidates, and 38 undergraduate workers. As projects have been completed, publication in the peer-reviewed literature has been very good creating a greater awareness in the academic community for issues of resource development. The total cost to MMS and LSU has been equal at $11,360,000 each. All of this has been achieved at a management cost of less than 2 percent.

Research tasks fell into five broad categories: Information Dissemination (4 projects at $1,325,000), Chemical Fates, Effects, and Bioremediation (13 projects at $2,053,000), Offshore Structure Ecology (6 projects at $2,807,000), Physical Oceanography and Meteorology (12 projects at $2,661,000), Deepwater Environment Studies (4 projects at $810,000), and Socioeconomics and Policy (16 projects at $2,225,000).

TABLE OF CONTENTS

1 INTRODUCTION

1.1 The Establishment of a Coastal Marine Institute by Minerals Management Service at Louisiana State University

The Minerals Management Service (MMS) of the U.S. Dept. of the Interior is charged with the management of ocean floor mineral resources in the Outer Continental Shelf (OCS) lying from 3 to 200 nautical miles offshore. Through MMS' Environmental Studies Program (ESP) numerous studies have been conducted since 1973 upon many aspects of the OCS and adjacent environments to provide information for management decisions. MMS anticipates future information needs reflecting new patterns of OCS development and new concerns. Since OCS utilization and concerns are region specific, and since MMS information needs overlap those of the State of Louisiana, a new mechanism has been adopted to support high quality research utilizing the best facilities and expertise in regions of high OCS activity.

The Center for Coastal Energy and Environmental Resources (CCEER) at LSU was designated a Coastal Marine Institute by joint agreement of MMS and the State of Louisiana. Negotiations were begun in 1991, and the first awards under an initial cooperative agreement were made in the fall of 1993. As the LSU CMI reached the end of the initial 5 years of operation, the agreement was extended an additional year while the scope of a second phase was being considered. The last award under this extended agreement was made in Jan 1999. Subsequently, a second cooperative agreement was signed that extends the LSU CMI in essentially the same form for an additional 5 years.

CMI is intended as a flexible funding avenue that encourages innovation, local participation, cofunding of projects and participation by individuals and smaller teams of investigators. However, the objectives of CMI sponsored projects differ little from regular MMS projects supported by the Environmental Studies Programs, and are useful in making management decisions. Typically, these decisions deal with the ecological risks and socioeconomic impacts. CMI projects are funded as task orders from MMS, and a MMS Contracting Officer's Technical Representative from the New Orleans Regional Office is assigned to each task order. There will be the usual emphasis upon high quality research both in reference to technical performance and innovation. Publication in peer reviewed journals is expected. Collaboration with and funding of graduate students is strongly encouraged in CMI projects.

1.2 CMI Objectives and Framework Issues

The LSU CMI program was established with six joint objectives as listed below:

1   respond to MMS, State, and local information needs and interests with local expertise of national caliber residing in an OCS region major research university;

2   enhance recognition and comprehension of study results through performance and presentation of results by a highly credible local research institution;

3   enhance existing local capabilities and facilities for innovative scientific research relevant to OCS resource management issues;

1

4   utilize the interdisciplinary environment of a research university to foster process oriented studies, needed technologies and concepts, and syntheses of information of greater utility to management;

5   achieve consensus between MMS and the various Louisiana departments with coastal and marine environmental resources responsibilities regarding the most important State information needs to be researched; and

6   reduce the costs to both the State and MMS of obtaining resource management information by cofunding information acquisition activities.

In order to select projects that helped meet these broad objectives, more specific framework topics were selected. These were intended to provide broad boundaries for guidance of the CMI in the development of specific research projects. Over the course of six years, the framework topics became relatively standardized and broad. A typical list might include:

(1) environmental aspects of technologies for extracting and transporting non-energy resources; (2) environmental response to changing energy extraction and transport technologies; (3) analyses and synthesis of existing data/information from previous studies; (4) modeling of environmental, social, and economic processes and systems; (5) new information about the structure/function of affected systems via application of descriptive and experimental means; and (6) projects which improve the application and distribution of multi-source information.

1.3   Project Statistics

The total contracted costs to MMS for CMI-I is $11,360,000, only slightly below the targeted amount of $2 million per year considered in the cooperative agreement. Failure to meet the targeted amount has three sources that are difficult to cleanly separate. First, in some years MMS selected fewer projects due to the lack of a large number of MMS-relevant proposals. Second, in some years MMS selected fewer projects due to insufficient funding. Third, in some years LSU submitted fewer MMS-relevant proposals due to a lack of matching opportunities.

It is especially noteworthy that only $209,000 was expended on CMI operations at LSU. This was less than 2 percent of the total amount awarded. Such a low management cost was possible due to LSU cost sharing, the restriction of CMI staff to part-time only, and transfer to routine grant administration to the University. Arguably, these cost-saving strategies resulted in a CMI management with only limited ability to track over 50 projects.

LSU provided at least 1:1 match on all projects. At the time of negotiation of the CMI-I cooperative agreement, it was anticipated that LSU would be provided with five year matching funds from the State legislature. Endorsement by two governors and two university chancellors proved, unfortunately, inadequate through years of shifting university priorities, rules for seeking support, and budget shortfalls. As a result, CMI met its matching obligations in an ad hoc manner. Departmental salary support was the primary source of match, followed by industry in-kind, and University-level funds. The industry in-kind was mostly in the form of logistical support for platform ecology studies.

Attempts were made to obtain cash match from industry, but that potential source was found to be unreliable.

1.4 Training of Students

It was the Stated desire of MMS that students be trained during the course of the research tasks. This has been done. At a minimum, CMI has influenced 38undergraduate workers, 22 master's students, 26 doctoral students, and 14 postdoctoral associates. That these are minimum figures stems from the fact that students supported by separately accounted departmental funds and fellowships have also worked on the project.

1.5 Participation of Faculty

A total for sixty-four faculty were listed as PI's or Co-PI's on CMI projects. These ranged from senior department chairs to the most recent junior hires. In two cases, CMI has effectively exhausted the available talent pool. This is the case for physical oceanography in which all LSU physical oceanographers have had at least one project. It is also the case in sociology where all relevant faculty in that department has been supported.

While most researchers on the project are at LSU, other participating institutions are:

Louisiana Universities Marine Research Consortium (LUMCON), University of New Orleans, Southeast Louisiana University, University of Louisiana at Lafayette, University of Southern Mississippi, Texas A&M University, Texas A&M at Corpus Christi, and Old Dominion, Virginia.

1.6 An Assessment of Effectiveness

The first six years of the LSU CMI can be judged to be highly effective by several different criteria. The most appropriate assessment, however, lies in examining how well the initial objectives have been met. Each can be considered separately.

1. Respond to needs and interests with local expertise of national caliber residing in an OCS region major research university.

   The LSU community and cooperating institutions has responded in an outstanding manner. Over sixty researchers have received CMI support ranging from well-known senior scientists to the newest postdoctoral associate.

2. Enhance recognition and comprehension of study results through performance and presentation of results by a highly credible local research institution.

   The results of completed projects are being published in the peer-reviewed literature at a rate of about three publications per task. In addition, the projects have been widely presented at national meetings.

3. Enhance existing local capabilities and facilities for innovative scientific research relevant to OCS resource management issues.

   Since the CMI agreement specifically excluded facility development, this objective was more difficult to meet, but it was met. In terms of people, LSU has been able to augment its tenure-track faculty with CMI-funded research

3

faculty. In terms of facilities, University matching funds have contributed significantly to development of the Louisiana Population Data Center and field-deployable oceanographic instrumentation.

4. Utilize the interdisciplinary environment of a research university to foster process oriented studies, needed technologies and concepts, and syntheses of information of greater utility to management.

   LSU's response has been outstanding. Smaller projects a have been undertaken in many separate departments, and large projects are multi-PI and include several departments.

5. Achieve consensus between MMS and the various Louisiana departments with coastal and marine environmental resources responsibilities regarding the most important State information needs to be researched.

   This is the one area where LSU's CMI has met with something less that great success. Initially envisioned as having cash match from the State, it was planned for appropriate agencies to help formally identify project priorities. Since LSU provides the great bulk of the match, the input from agencies is less formally obtained. CMI has on a few occasions, however allowed MMS to be quickly responsive to new needs put forward by the State.

6. Reduce the costs to both the State and MMS of obtaining resource management.

   Again great success has been obtained. The actual cost of the CMI projects is twice that which MMS has paid.

1.7   List of Studies Completed Under the CMI: From 1992 - 1998

1. Outer Continental Shelf Issues: Central Gulf of Mexico – Task 19902 – OCS Study MMS 95-0032

2. Characteristics and Possible Impacts of a Restructured OCS Oil and Gas Industry in the Gulf of Mexico – Task 19903 – OCS Study MMS 95-055

3. Development and Application of the Sublethal Toxicity Test to PAH Using Marine Harpacticoid Copepods – Task 19905 – OCS Study MMS 99-0001

4. Modeling the Structure and Performance of Integrated and Independent Producers in the Gulf of Mexico OCS Region – Task 19906 – OCS Study MMS 95-0056

5. Effect of Produced-Water Discharge on Bottom Sediment Chemistry, Final Report – Task 19907 – OCS Study MMS 99-0060

6. Numerical Simulation of Gulf of Mexico Circulation Under Present and Glacial Climatic Conditions Task 19908 – OCS Study MMS 96-0067

7. Improved Geohazards and Benthic Habitat Evaluations: Digital Acoustic Data with Ground Truth Calibrations – Task 19910 – OCS Study MMS 2001-050

8. Wave Climate Modeling and Evaluation Relative to Sand Mining on Ship Shoal, Offshore Louisiana, for Coastal and Barrier Island Restoration, Final Report – Task 19911 – OCS Study MMS 96-0059

9. Wave Climate and Bottom Boundary Layer Dynamics with Implications for Offshore Sand Mining and Barrier Island Replenishment in South-Central Louisiana – Task 19911 – OCS Study MMS 2000-053

10. Seasonal and Spatial Variation in the Biomass and Size Frequency Distribution of Fish Associated with Oil and Gas Platforms in the Northern Gulf of Mexico – Task 19915 – OCS Study MMS 2000-05

11. Development and Characterization of Sea Anemones as Bioindicators of Offshore Resource Exploitation and Environmental Impact – Task 19916 – OCS Study MMS 99-0037

12. Coastal Marine Environmental Modeling – Task 19917 – OCS Study MMS 98-052

13. Assessment of PAH Composition of Diesel Fuel Absorbed to Marine Sediments and Their Toxicity to Aquatic Food Webs – Task 19919 – OCS Study MMS 98-0057

14. Biodegradation of Aromatic Heterocycles from Petroleum Produced-Water and Pyrogenic Sources in Marine Sediments – Task 19920 – OCS Study MMS 2000-060

15. Environmental and Safety Risks of an Expanding Role for Independents on the Gulf of Mexico OCS – Task 19923 – OCS Study MMS 98-0021

16. Effects of Oil and Gas Development: A Current Awareness Bibliography – Task 19924 – OCS Study MMS 97-0045

17. Analysis of Ambient Pollutant Concentrations and Meteorological Conditions Affecting EPA Class I and II Areas in Southeastern Louisiana, Volume I: Technical Report – Task 19925 – OCS Study MMS 96-0062

18. Analysis of Ambient Pollutant Concentrations and Meteorological Conditions Affecting EPA Class I and II Areas in Southeastern Louisiana, Volume II: Appendices – Task 19925 – OCS Study MMS 96-0063

19. Long-Term Measurements of SO2 and NO2 Concentrations and Related Meterological Conditions in the Northeast Gulf of Mexico, Interim Report – Task 19925 – OCS 98-0020

20. Air Quality and Dispersion Meteorology over the Northeastern Gulf of Mexico: Measurements, Analyses, and Syntheses – Task 19925 – OCS Study MMS 2000-014

21. Potential for Accelerated Bioremediation and Restoration of Oil-Impacted Marshes through the Selection of Superior Oil-Tolerant Vegetation – Task 19927 – OCS Study MMS 2000-042

22. Coastal Currents in the Northern Gulf of Mexico, Dixie County, Florida, to the U.S.-Mexico Border – Task 19928 – OCS Study MMS 97-0005

23. Studying and Verifying the Use of Chemical Biomarkers for Identifying and Quantitating Oil Residues in the Environment –Task 19933 – OCS Study MMS 2000-086

24. Forecasting the Number of Offshore Platforms on the Gulf of Mexico OCS to the Year 2023 – Task 19934 – OCS Study MMS 2001-013

25. Long-term Effects of Contaminants from OCS Produced-water Discharges at Pelican Island Facility, Louisiana –Task 19937 – OCS Study MMS 98-0039

26. Wind and Eddy Related Circulation on the Louisiana/Texas Shelf and Slope Determined from Satellite and In-Situ Measurements: October 1993-August 1994 –Task 19942 – OCS Study MMS 2001-025

27. Lafourche Parish and Port Fourchon, Louisiana: Effects of the Outer Continental Shelf Petroleum Industry on the Economy and Public Services, Part 1 –Task 19945 – OCS Study MMS 2001-019

28. Fate and Effects of Barium and Radium-Rich Fluid Emissions from Hydrocarbon Seeps on the Benthic Habitats of the Gulf of Mexico Offshore Louisiana – Task 19946 – OCS Study MMS 2001-004

29. Dynamic Height and Seawater Transport across the Texas-Louisiana Shelf Break – Task 19948 – OCS Study MMS 2000-045

30. Effects of Oil and Gas Development: A Current Awareness Bibliography – Task 19950 – OCS Study MMS 2000-083

31. Economic and Social Consequences of the Oil Spill in Lake Barre, Louisiana – Task 19955 – OCS Study MMS 99-028

2 Research Topic Summaries and Task Listings

2.1 Research Area: Information Dissemination

Four tasks that can be grouped into two projects have been supported in the area of information dissemination. The first such project (tasks 19924 and 19950), "Effects of Offshore Oil and Gas Development: A Current Awareness Bibliography" was initiated at LUMCON under the URI and is ongoing. It provides MMS and interested parties with a quarterly listing of relevant publications, about 100 references a quarter. When copies are available for review, a brief informative abstract is given.

Two other CMI projects (tasks 19901 and 19964) have been important components in MMS's development of a Gulf-Wide Geographic Information System (G-WIS). These projects are "Design and Development of an Environmental GIS to Support Oil Spill Contingency Planning & Environmental Analysis in the Northern Gulf of Mexico" and a follow on " Development of Louisiana GIS Data in Support of the MMS Gulf-wide Information System. Planning for G-WIS preceded the establishment of CMI. During the first year of three CMI programs, the feasibility of developing a Gulf-wide program trough CMI was explored. It was concluded, however, that the administrative restrictions of the CMI agreement made such comprehensive development unfeasible. The follow-on CMI project, therefore, was restricted to Louisiana contributions to the G-WIS effort.

2.1.1 Design and Development of an Environmental GIS to Support Oil Spill Contingency Planning & Environmental Analysis in the Northern Gulf of Mexico Task 19901

Principal Investigators: Shea Penland (currently at University of New Orleans) and Linda Wayne

Project Status: Completed.

MMS Relevance: The Gulf-Wide Information System offers MMS and other resource planners a simple, efficient, and effective means of accessing all available information bearing upon environmental decisions. Initiated for the limited purpose of oil spill response planning, G-WIS can serve as a model for a much broader range of oil and gas development issues. This particular task had dual purposes. First, it served as a developmental environment for the larger G-WIS. Second, it began development of the Louisiana portion of the data set.

Project Description: The Gulf-Wide Information System (G-WIS) is a cooperative effort between Louisiana State University (LSU) and the U.S. Minerals Management Service (MMS) to develop a geographic database to support oil spill contingency planning in the U.S. Gulf of Mexico. The objectives of the project are to develop a regionally complete and consistent GIS database from Florida to Texas that can be used for oil spill planning (not response) as well as for other environmental and computer applications. The enhanced ESI concept includes additional items in the database, expanded offshore geographic coverage, metadata for each geographic feature, information on level of effort and area covered by surveys, and procedures to assure regional consistency and completeness. The objective is to have G-WIS serve as a model and a first step toward developing a flexible and complete Gulf of Mexico database based on primary data.

The G-WIS database is described using four categories of information.

1. Reference: including bathymetry, directional currents, shoreline, hydrography, salinity, tides/water level, water temperature, elevation contours, wave height, and wind direction.

2. Human-Use: including population, land use, navigation aids, navigation channels, place names, transportation, and utilities.

3. Administrative: including Federal leasing areas, State leasing areas, managed lands, political boundaries, protraction areas, and regulated areas.

4. Biology: including birds, fish, habitats, mammals, nests, reptiles, shellfish, and survey boundaries.

These data layers may each contain numerous sub-layers (coverages).

LSU established a laboratory facility on campus to house needed equipment and personnel. The laboratory was comprised of information technology including a large capacity Unix-based server, Sun SPARC workstations, personal computers, digitizing equipment, and a hardcopy map plotter. Primary software products included ESRI Arc/Info geographic information system (GIS), ERDAS GIS and image processing software, and Oracle relational data base management system. Access to the system was provided via Internet. The laboratory was staffed by a team of computer scientists, remote sensing/GIS analysts, and environmental scientists.

The information laboratory staff was responsible for locating, assessing, collecting, compiling, documenting, and managing the oil spill contingency planning data resources. The staff was responsible for the translation of existing digital data resources to a common geographic base, digitizing non-digital data resources, and the derivation of needed information from existing digital resources such as imagery. Program staff devised and implemented programs for quality control, data tracking, and data documentation. All data included within the program met Federal digital data standards including the Spatial Data Transfer Standard (SDTS) and the emerging data documentation (metadata) standard.

Student Participation: Undergraduate 1, Graduate Joel Register and Srinivasa Lingenini

Publications: Not applicable.

2.1.2 Development of Louisiana GIS Data in Support of the MMS Gulf-wide Information System (G-WIS) Task 19964

Principal Investigators: Lynda Wayne and DeWitt Braud

Project Status: Ongoing

MMS Relevance: The Gulf-Wide Information System offers MMS and other resource planners a simple, efficient, and effective means of accessing all available information bearing upon environmental decisions. Initiated for the limited purpose of oil spill response planning, G-WIS can serve as a model for a much broader range of oil and gas development issues. This particular task provides Louisiana data to the larger effort. This task is effectively a continuation of the initial MMS-CMI planning G-WIS project and has the same MMS relevance. G-WIS will afford MMS and various State agencies immediate access to all relevant information needed in oil spill contingency planning and actual response. This task develops the data layers needed specifically for the State of Louisiana.

Project Description: This project is the completion of work begun during the initial CMI participation in G-WIS. The primary objectives are:

1. locate best available data resources

2. enhance and convert existing information into G-WIS specified digital format

3. develop new data sets for missing or obsolete information

4. make all data available to the MMS, industry, and the public via the internet or other MMS-specified management system.

The specific data areas are:

1. Environmental Sensitivity Index (ESI) data relative to birds, nests, mammals, fish, reptiles, invertebrates, habitats, and socioeconomic activities.

2. Geophysical data including bathymetry, topography, imagery, hydrography, USGS quadrangle Index.

3. Human-use data including place names and transportation

4. Administrative data including State lease areas, managed lands, political boundaries, and regulated areas.

Student Participation: Undergraduate: two undergraduate students are employed, Graduate: two graduate students are employed

Publications: Not applicable

2.1.3 Current Awareness Bibliography Tasks 19924 and 19950

Principal Investigators: Nancy Rabalais and Mike Dagg

Status: Ongoing, continuous since initiation under URI.

MMS Relevance: MMS resource managers are faced with the need the content of a rapidly increasing body of information. The most effective way to make this literature tractable is to provide an annotated bibliography. This CMI task does this very thing.

Project Description: The current LUMCON - MMS) quarterly annotated bibliography, titled *Effects of Offshore Oil and Gas Development,* has been addressing OCS and coastal marine issues since 1990. Started under the MMS University Research Initiative URI, the project has been continued under CMI. Thirty-eight issues have been distributed. The current distribution list numbers three hundred and twenty.

The bibliography is prepared with the objective of being a relevant contribution to the MMS - LSU CMI program by responding to varied information needs, contributing to the inter-disciplinary environment of the CMI, assisting in achieving consensus between

MMS and various Louisiana departments and improving the application and distribution of multi-source information.

Anticipated future enhancement includes electronic distribution of the quarterly bibliography and development of a searchable Internet database. However, many features will remain consistent with the current hard-copy format to provide continuity from the prior bibliography. This will make the entire database, from 1990 on, readily accessible to MMS LSU CMI investigators and contractors. While the bibliography is prepared to serve the information needs of the MMS - LSU CMI program, it is distributed to all recipients of the current bibliography and anyone else who requests it.

The bibliography is prepared at the Louisiana Universities Marine Consortium LUMCON) Library, by the Librarian (position vacant at this time) who is given scientific and technical support from Dr. Mike Dagg, Professor at LUMCON. Mr. Hooper-Lane and Dr. Dagg will be further supported by the LUMCON Library Assistant, the Computer Engineer and one undergraduate assistant (0.5 FIE) per summer.

Student Involvement: One student assistant.

2.2 Research Area: Chemical Fates, Effects, and Bioremediation

Twelve projects were initiated in the area of chemical fates, effects, and bioremediation at a cost to MMS of $2,053,000 and a similar match from LSU. Two sought improved methods of assaying for sublethal impacts (task 19905 using amphipods and task 19916 using sea anemones). Three examined degradation pathways (tasks 19907, 19920, and 19933). Two examined longer-term contamination on a single-decade scale (task 19937) and on a multi-decade scale (task 19930). One examined and found correct the old conjecture that coastal Louisiana ecosystems are adapted to chronic oiling (task 19914), while another looked at the possibility of population genetic impacts in the benthos (task 19949). One also looked at the ecosystem response of foodwebs to oiling (task 19919).

While several of the tasks addressed issues pertinent to bioremediation, two were especially focused on that topic. Task 19909 made use of a historic marsh spill to explore improved remediation. Task 19927 identified strains of marsh grass most tolerant of post-spill conditions.

2.2.1 Development and Application of Sub-lethal Toxicity Tests on PAH Using Harpacticoid Copepods Task 19905

Principal Investigator: John W. Fleeger

Status: Completed, report issued.

Fleeger, J.W. and G.R. Lotufo. Development and application of a sublethal toxicity test to PAH using marine harpacticoid copepods: Final report. OCS Study MMS Pub. No. MMS 99-0001. U.S. Dept. of the Interior, Minerals Management Service, Gulf of Mexico OCS Region, New Orleans, Louisiana, 38pp.

MMS Relevance - Traditional methods of detecting impacts on invertebrate fauna have depended upon benthic sampling and species inventory. Unfortunately, it is very difficult to establish a link between inventory numbers and sublethal impacts. Therefore, unambiguous assays are needed. Dr. Fleeger proposed to develop such an assay with a common component of benthic systems, harpacticoid copepods. These are an excellent assay organism in that they carry an egg clutch that can be used to determine reproductive output.

Project Summary - The marine environment has been subjected to heavy contamination of polynuclear aromatic hydrocarbons (PAH). The goal of this project is to develop a sub-lethal toxicity test as a biomarker for PAH using harpacticoid copepods as test organisms. Harpacticoids live near or at the sediment-water interface, ranging from estuaries to the outer continental shelf, and play a significant role in food webs. They are also sensitive organisms for assessing the effects of pollutants. This standardized test will measure PAH effects on survival and reproduction. A known number of gravid females of several species of salt marsh harpacticoids will be exposed to different concentrations of sediment-bound PAH from two sources (a mix of selected PAH and diesel fuel). After one generation, the reproductive output (number of larvae and juveniles produced) will be determined. Acute toxicity tests ($96hLC_{50}$) will also be conducted with all the species investigated. Performing a standardized test will facilitate the generation of data with important management implications.

A successful bioassay was developed. Test protocols yielded repeatable results and statistically sound data. Adult harpacticoids were found to be relatively tolerant to PAHs in 10-day exposures. Species-specific differences in sensitivity were detected. Early life history stages were much more sensitive than adults in one species but not in the other. Low concentrations of PAHs decreased copepod offspring production, egg hatching success, and embryonic and early-stage development, demonstrating the high sensitivity of life history related endpoints. In addition, grazing on microalgae was significantly impaired at low concentrations after short exposures (< 30 h). Finally it was demonstrated that harpacticoids could actively avoid contamination. These protocols are proving useful to address other questions regarding contaminant effects on benthic organisms. The results of the life history studies suggest that, for S. knabeni, offspring production is the most sensitive life-cycle variable, followed probably by age at first reproduction and egg hatching success. For N. lacustris, results suggest that survivorship at the copepodite stages is the most sensitive variable, followed by offspring production, and egg hatching.

Student Participation: Graduate Students Guilherme R. Lotufo, Ph.D, undergraduates 3.

Publications:

Lotufo G. R. 1998. Lethal and sublethal toxicity of sediment-associated fluoranthene to benthic copepods: Application of the critical-body-residue approach. Aquat. Toxicol. 44: 17-30.

Lotufo G. R. 1998. Bioaccumulation of sediment-associated fluoranthene in benthic copepods: uptake, elimination and biotransformation. Aquat. Toxicol. 44: 1-15.

Lotufo G. R. and J. W. Fleeger. 1997. Effects of sediment-associated phenanthrene on survival, development and reproduction of two species of meiobenthic copepods. Mar. Ecol. Prog. Ser. 151: 91-102.

Lotufo G. R. 1997. Toxicity of sediment-associated PAHs to an estuarine copepod: effects on survival, feeding, reproduction and behavior. Mar. Environ. Res. 44: 149-166.

2.2.2 Role of Bottom Sediment Redox-Chemistry Near Oil Production Facilities on the Sequester/Release and/or Degradation of Metals, Radionuclides, and Organics Task 19907

Principal Investigators: R.D. Delaune, J.H. Pardue, W.J. Catallo, and C.W. Lindau

Status: Completed final report issued.

DeLaune, R.D., C.W. Lindau, and R.P. Gambrell. 1999. Role of bottom sediment redox-chemistry near oil production facilities on the sequester/release and/or degradation of metals, radionuclides and organics: northern Gulf of Mexico. U.S. Dept. of the Interior, Minerals Management Service, Gulf of Mexico OCS Region, New Orleans. LA, and the U.S. Dept. of the Interior, Metarie Office. OCS Study MMS 99-0060. 47pp.

MMS Relevance: Estuarine regions exposed to OCS discharges are a geochemically complex systems where the fate and effects of discharged material and possible remediation are dependant upon the system dynamics. If MMS is to anticipate the effect of coastal discharge, it is necessary to understand the control exerted by the geochemical system. This study began with the knowledge that the transition from oxygenated to anoxic conditions is the predominant geochemical gradient of considerable ecological consequence, and sought to determine processes across that gradient that influenced pollutants.

Project Summary: Petroleum hydrocarbons, metals and radionuclides can or have entered the environment surrounding Louisiana's on-shore and near-shore oil and gas production and recovery operations. In the proposed research the sediment geochemical properties governing the sequester/release of metals and radionuclides or degradation of petroleum hydrocarbons were quantified. The influence of sediment redox pH conditions on the speciation, solubility and mobility of the contaminant were evaluated. Models were developed for predicting the importance of the observed range in sediment geochemical properties on either retention, transport or degradation of these pollutants.

In this study, the kinetics and transformations of heavy metals, radium, and petroleum hydrocarbon degradation in estuarine sediment at a site in Coastal Louisiana receiving produced water discharge were examined. The effects of sediment redox potential (Eh) on the kinetics of transformation of toxic metals and radium in sediments are detailed. Petroleum hydrocarbon degradation was also studied. Studies were designed to determine the speciation and solubility of heavy metals in sediment receiving produced water discharge. Sediment was collected from a canal (Humble Canal) from a waste pit at the point of discharge associated with a petroleum recovery operation in the Lirette Oil and Gas field in Terrebonne Parish. The effluent or produced water was discharged from the secondary compartment of the pit into the canal. Five active wells contributed produced water to the pit. Average discharge has been reported to be 482 barrels per day. The sediment had a pH=7.0 and contained 0.1 percent Ba, 0.04 percent Mn and 2 percent

Fe. The heavy metal content of the sediment was determined using wet ashing and ICP procedures.

The effect of sediment redox conditions on the solubility behavior of Fe, Pb, Ni, Ba, and Cu in bottom sediment collected from a produced water discharge site was investigated using kinetics and chemical fractionation procedures. Kinetics and chemical fractionation procedures were also used in quantifying the effects of sediment redox (Eh) condition on the behaviors of As, Cd, Cr and Zn in the bottom sediment collected from a Louisiana Coastal site receiving produced water discharge. Sediment samples were incubated in microcosms in which Eh-pH conditions were controlled. Sediment was sequentially extracted for metals in various chemical fractions (water soluble, exchangeable, bound to carbonates, bound to iron and manganese oxides, bound to insoluble organic and sulfides) and chemical inactive fraction (mineral residue).

Sediment from oil recovery pit and stream bottom sediment receiving produced water discharge were incubated in laboratory microcosm under oxidized and reduced sediment conditions. The sediment was then extracted into various fractions and analyzed for radium-226. The results indicated that very little (5 percent) of the total radium in the sediment material was present in a form that was extractable or otherwise available from the waste-pit material and/or bottom sediment (such forms include water-soluble, exchangeable, associated with carbonates, reducible, or organic/sulfide). Approximately 95 percent of the radium present were tied up in a residual form that could be extracted only with very strong acids. Radium in this fraction would be released very slowly into the environment from the contaminated sediment.

Rate of petroleum hydrocarbon degradation was measured in sediment collected from a low energy brackish wetland site which had been exposed for a number of years to produced water discharge. Recalcitrant or higher molecular weight compounds were the primary hydrocarbon fractions found in the sediment. Degradation rates were determined by measuring loss of selected petroleum hydrocarbon components with time in laboratory incubation. South Louisiana Crude oil was added to the sediment to measure degradation rates of soluble hydrocarbons that were too low in concentration in the original sediment. Oxidized sediment conditions resulted in a higher rate of degradation for most hydrocarbon fractions as compared to reduced sediment. Fertilizer or nutrient amendments to contaminated sediments significantly increased the rate of hydrocarbon degradation. Fertilizer enhanced the degradation of the lower and more soluble molecular weight fractions as compared to the higher molecular weight fractions.

Heavy metal solubility was shown to be low in anaerobic and neutral pH estuarine sediment found at a coastal Louisiana produced water discharge sties. Solubility of Ba found in barite was low under alkaline and either anaerobic or aerobic sediment conditions. Over 95 percent of radium found in contaminated sediment existed as an unavailable form that could be extracted only with strong acids. Typical heavy metal pollution levels found in the surface sediment environment at produced water discharge sites would not impact microbial degradation of petroleum hydrocarbons in the sediment column. Oxidized sediment conditions resulted in a faster rate of petroleum hydrocarbon degradation as compared to reducing sediment conditions in a produced water impacted sediment column.

Student Participation: Undergraduate workers - 4. Grad Students: Bradley Banker (MS), Debra Woodall (MS), and Tingzong Guo (Ph.D)

Publications:

DeLaune, R.D., C.W. Lindau, B.C. Banker, and I. Devai. In Press. Degradation of petroleum hydrocarbons in sediment receiving produced water discharge. J. Environmental Science and Health

Carbonell, A.A., M.A. Aarabi, R.D. DeLaune, R.P. Gambrell, W.H. Patrick Jr. 1998. Arsenic in wetland vegetation: availability, phytotoxicity, uptake and effects on plant growth and nutrition. The Science of the Total Environment 217:189-199.

Guo, Tingzong, R.D. DeLaune, and W.H. Patrick Jr. 1997. The effect of sediment redox chemistry on solubility/chemically active forms of selected metals in bottom sediment receiving produced water discharge. Spill Science and Technology Bulletin 4:165-175.

Guo, Tingzong, R.D. DeLaune, and W.H. Patrick Jr. 1997. The influence of sediment redox chemistry on chemically active forms of arsenic, cadmium, chromium, and zinc in estuarine sediment. Environment International 23:305-316.

Carbonell, A.A., R. Pulido, R.D. DeLaune, and W.H. Patrick Jr. 1999. Soluble barium in barite and phosphogypsum amended Mississippi River alluvial sediment. Journal of Environmental Quality 28:316-321.

DeLaune, R.D. and R.P. Gambrell. Role of sediment in isolating metal contaminants in wetland environments. Journal of Environmental Science and Health A31:2349-2362.

DeLaune, R.D., W.H. Patrick and T./ Guo. 1998. The redox-pH chemistry of chromium in water and sediment. IN H.E. Allen, A.W. Garrison, and G.W. Luther III eds. Metals in Surface Waters. Sleeping Bear Press. Pp 241-255.

DeLaune, R.D., C. Mulbah, I. Devai, and C.W. Lindau. 1998. Effect of chromium and lead on degradation of south Louisiana crude oil in sediment. Journal of Environmental Science and Health A33:527-546.

Woodwell, D.W. 1998. Tracking oil and gas produced water in an open water estuarine system using salinity as a conservative tracer. A MS thesis in Oceanography and Coastal Sciences at Louisiana State University.

Guo, Tingzong, 1995. Biogeochemistry of toxic materials in wetlands. Ph.D. thesis in Oceanography and Coastal Sciences. Louisiana State University.

Banker, B.C. 1996. Environmental influences on petroleum hydrocarbons degradation in sediment at a produced water discharge site. A M.S. thesis in Agronomy at Louisiana State University.

2.2.3 The Development of Bioremediation for Oil Spill Cleanup in Coastal Wetlands Task 19909

Principal Investigators: Irving A. Mendelssohn, Qianxin Lin, Karolien Debusschere, Charles B. Henry Jr, Edward B. Overton, S. Penland, Ralph J. Portier, Nancy N. Rabalais, and Maud M. Walsh

Status: An Industry Cooperation Project with Mobil Inc. Started Cycle I, final report pending.

MMS Relevance: Remediation technology is a rapidly advancing area attracting academic and industrial interest from many disciplines. Products intended to accelerate degradation of spilled oils are now commercially available, but their effectiveness in the full remediation process is too poorly known for MMS to endorse their application. This project examines bacterial seeding under controlled laboratory and field conditions to test effects upon flora, fauna, and microbiota in a coastal system.

Project Summary: Wetlands are fragile environments that when subjected to oil spills are often more impacted by cleanup attempts than by the oil itself. A need, therefore, exists to develop less intrusive methods by which spilled petroleum hydrocarbons can be efficiently removed from the wetland environment a means by which oil released into coastal wetlands, as well as other wetland types, may be remedied.

This project is a comprehensive, multi-disciplinary experimental program to test the use of both microbial seeding (with bacteria selected for high rates of oil degradation) and fertilizers (to enhance natural biodegradation) as a means of oil spill cleanup In coastal salt marshes. We propose to use both controlled greenhouse experiments as well as field trials to test the efficacy and ecological safety of these enhanced biodegradation methodologies. This proposed three-year study is designed to test the following aspects of bioremediation in coastal marshes:

     (1)   Product Toxicity: Determine if the maximum allowable loading rate (as defined by the product manufacturer) of the selected bioremediation products generates adverse impacts to wetland plants, infaunal animals and microbial communities. This experiment is required to ensure that the product-loading rate suggested by the manufacturer is not toxic to wetland plants and estuarine animals. Only products on the National Contingency Plan (NCP) list, with defined maximum loading rates, will be used in this study.

     (2)   Biodegradation Potential: Determine the effect of fertilizer and microbial seeding on oil biodegradation in salt marsh soil mesocosms. This experiment is essential to determine the potential for enhanced oil biodegradation via bioremediation in salt marsh substrates and is the first step before large-scale field trials. We shall also determine if it is the microbial component, per se, of the seeding product that is actually responsible for enhanced biodegradation.

     (3)   Marsh Soil Type: Determine to what extent product-enhanced oil biodegradation is modified by marsh soil type. Salt marsh soils, depending on their texture and specific microbial communities, may exhibit different capacities for bioremediation which must be quantified in order to access the variability in bioremediation potential of salt marshes.

(4)   Product Reapplication: Determine (a) if product reapplication is required to maintain an enhanced rate of biodegradation and, thus, to maximize total hydrocarbon degradation and (1)) whether reapplication rate is a function of initial oil dosage. Reapplication of the fertilizer bioremediation product is likely during a real cleanup operation. Thus, the efficacy of reapplication as a means of maintaining maximum biodegradation rates at different oil dosing levels will be evaluated.

(5)   Field Bioremediation Trial: Determine, under real-world conditions, the degree to which the potential for bioremediation demonstrated in the greenhouse marsh mesocosms is realized in the field. This experiment will be designed to assess bioremediation in both streamside salt marshes, where subsurface hydrology is a relatively active, and immediately adjacent inland salt marshes, where subsurface hydrology is minimal. Both bioremediation efficacy and ecological safety will be evaluated.

The proposed research will be the first comprehensive investigation of the efficacy and safety of bioremediation in the coastal salt marsh habitat. The results of this research will generate an answer to the question: Is bioremediation, via fertilization and/or microbial seeding, an effective and ecologically safe means of oil spill cleanup in coastal wetlands? An answer to this question is strongly needed in order to reduce the impact of oil spill cleanup in the sensitive wetland environment.

Student Participation: Post Doctoral Dr. Qianxin Lin

Publications:

Lin, Q. et. al. In press. Effects of bioremediation agents on oil degradation in mineral and sandy sediments. Environmental Toxicology

2.2.4   Are Coastal Fauna Chronically Exposed to Petroleum Hydrocarbons and Hypoxia Better Adapted to These Factors? Task 19914

Principal Investigator: William B. Stickle

Status: Completed, final report pending revision.

MMS Relevance - The unequivocal detection of environmental impact in the ocean environment is an extremely difficult challenge to sampling design since that environment experiences great natural variation which can mask or confound man-caused changes. This fact has given rise to much of the valid scientific criticism of MMS studies. In the Gulf of Mexico there is even an additional problem of impact detection; the impact may have been chronic before studies begin. Dr. Stickle addresses this possibility for the Louisiana coast by direct comparison of invertebrate physiology from habitats with a varying history of oil development.

Project Summary - Coastal Louisiana has been impacted by oil field activities for the last half of the twentieth century and the waters over the continental shelf west of the Mississippi River Delta are also subject to extensive periods of hypoxia annually during the summer months known locally as dead water zones. In addition, hurricane activity and diurnal variation in dissolved oxygen stress the marine fauna. Yet these same waters annually produce large catches of shrimp and blue crabs. This project is designed to address two questions: (1) Is there a synergism between exposure to the water soluble-

16

fraction (WSF) of petroleum hydrocarbons and hypoxic water that alters the tolerance and physiological performance of coastal fauna?; and (2) Are animals with a long history of sublethal exposure to the WSF of petroleum hydrocarbons and hypoxia (over many generations) better adapted to those stresses than animals which have not been previously exposed to those conditions? Long-term tolerance studies (28 days) will be performed in the form of bioassays for both petroleum hydrocarbons and dissolved oxygen alone and in combination with two species of blue crabs, Callinectes sapidus (more estuarine) and C. similis (more marine) and the gulf killifish, Fundulus grandis. Sublethal indices of stress that will be used to assess animal condition are the RNA:DNA ratio as an instantaneous measure of growth rate and EROD activity p-450 enzyme system. Animals from an impacted locale as an index of petroleum hydrocarbon metabolizing capability by the (Barataria Bay, LA) and a putative pristine locale (northwest Florida near the Florida State Marine Laboratory) will be used to address the second question. The results of this study will provide managers with valuable information about the impact of oil exposure on marine animals under hypoxic conditions and the influence of prior exposure to petroleum hydrocarbons on animal tolerance and physiological performance.

Student Participation: One undergrad and Hiram Szeto (MS)

Publications:

Szeto, H. 1998. Ethoxyresorufin-o-deethylase induction and physiological indices in two populations of Fundulus grandis exposed to the water soluble fraction of crude oil. M.S. thesis, Louisiana State University (Baton Rouge, La.). Dept. of Zoology and Physiology. 84pp.

2.2.5 Development and Characterization of Sea Anemones as Bioindicators of Offshore Resource Exploitation and Environmental Impact Task 19916

Principal Investigator: Gary Winston and William Stickle

Status: Completed, final report issued.

Winston, G. W. and L.W. Heffernan.1999. Development and characterization of sea anemones as bioindicators of offshore resource exploitation and environmental impact. US Dept. of Interior Gulf of Mexico OCS Region, New Orleans. OCS Study MMS-99-0037. 102pp.

MMS Relevance - One highly successful means of determining if an organism has been stressed by exposure to hydrocarbons is to determine in stress-induced enzyme systems, called biomarkers, can be detected in the tissues. Unfortunately, from an ecological perspective, advances in biomarker technology are most advanced in vertebrate species. Therefore, the method is not applicable to the great diversity of invertebrates that dominate marine systems. If such biomarker assays could be developed for invertebrate, the utility of the technique would be greatly increased with respect to MMS' information needs. The project proved that biomarkers were induced in anemones.

Project Description: The goal of this research was to provide valid information on the use of biomarkers for early-(sublethal) detection of potentially deleterious environmental impact. As a representative to the *NATO Advanced Research Workshop on Biomarkers* the P1 is extensively involved in development of international protocols for the effective use of biomarkers. The basis of biomarker research was to establish quantifiable reproducibility of the responses of biochemical systems of organisms to environmental impact.

The work was extremely successful. The common coastal anemone from Louisiana, Bunodosoma cavernata was assayed along with a second Gulf species, Condylactis gigantea from the Florida Keys, and three better-studied species from the west coast, Anthopleura elegantissima, A. xanthogrammica, and Aiptasia pallida. Various assays and technique development efforts sought to determine if these invertebrates catalyze enzymatic monooxygenation of organic xenobiotics employing the cytochrome P540-dependent monooxygen system. Indeed, exposure to a polyaromatic hydrocarbon (PAH, benzo[a]pyrene) did induce species-dependent levels of the cytochrome P540 system. The responses were quantifiable using methods advanced in this study. It was also found that the enzyme system was induced by cadmium.

Student Participation: Graduate Linda Heffernan (Ph.D.), John Dugas (Ph.D), and 2 undergraduate workers.

Publication: None reported

2.2.6 Assessment of PAH Composition of Diesel Fuel Absorbed to Marine Sediments and Their Toxicity to Aquatic Food Webs Task 19919

Principal Investigator: Kevin Carman and Jay Means

Status: Completed, report issued

Carman, K.R and J.C. Means. 1998. Assessment of PAH composition of diesel fuel sorbed to marine sediments and their toxicity to aquatic food webs. OCS Study MMS 98-0057. U.S. Dept. of the Interior, Minerals Management Service, Gulf of Mexico OCS Region, New Orleans, Louisiana, 30 pp.

MMS Relevance: It has long been established that in laboratory bioassays a variety of organisms show marked toxic response to components of petroleum. However, it has never been completely clear how such lab trials equate with field conditions in terms of the nature of exposure, and the response at an ecosystem level. Seldom are studies of biological effects able to predict subtle, long-lasting ecological effects, especially in regards to functional interactions among organisms and trophic levels. Taking advantage of a mesocosm protocol and facility developed for the Office of Naval Research, this project gave MMS an indication of response to oiling at the bacterial base of the detritus foodweb in coastal marshes.

Project Summary: Polycyclic aromatic hydrocarbons (PAH) are a highly toxic group of compounds present in crude oil and many petroleum products. Estuarine salt marshes are critical marine habitat because of their high productivity and importance as nursery grounds for many commercially important species. They are susceptible to chronic and/or catastrophic inputs of petroleum hydrocarbons, such as PAH, because of the physical and geochemical character of salt marshes. OBJECTIVES: Our goal was to determine the influence of sublethal exposure to sediment-bound PAH on the physiological condition, activity, and abundance of sedimentary bacteria.

The microcosm experiment portion was carried out at the LUMCON Marine Education Center in Cocodrie, LA. The benthic community used in the microcosm experiment was obtained from a shallow creek-fed pond in the Terrebonne Bay estuary ($29^\circ15'$N; $91^\circ21'$W) adjacent to the LUMCON facility. Microcosms consisted of intact sediment samples that were collected by gently pushing 15.2-cm i.d. PVC pipe into marsh mud exposed at low tide. A base was placed on the microcosm, which was then transferred to the LUMCON facility and placed in one of four wet tables. Windows were cut in the side of microcosms and covered with Nitex mesh (62-µm) to allow exchange of water (but not meiofauna). Microcosms were placed in wet tables and irrigated with water pumped directly from the marsh near the LUMCON facility and illuminated with banks of fluorescent lights. Microcosms were treated with three levels of diesel-contaminated sediment. Uncontaminated sediment only was added to an additional set of microcosms and served as an "application control", i.e., a control for the process of adding contaminants to microcosms.

Rapid removal of PAH by bacteria suggests that even if the marsh were exposed to chronically high levels of petroleum hydrocarbons, chemical evidence of the contaminants would not be detected in sediments. Collectively, these results are consistent with the hypothesis that the bacterial community in this salt marsh has adapted to chronic exposure to petroleum hydrocarbons.

Diesel contaminants in microcosms as determined from polycyclic aromatic hydrocarbon (PAH) concentration ranged from 0.55 to 55 ppm (dry weight). Bacterial metabolism (incorporation of 14C-acetate and 3H-leucine) and bacterial abundance were not affected by diesel-contaminated sediment at any concentration. Bacterial degradation of 14C-phenanthrene, however, increased in direct proportion to the amount of diesel-contaminated sediment added. Ambient sediment also exhibited significant capacity to degrade PAH. The half-life of phenanthrene (based on 14C-phenanthrene-degradation experiments) ranged from 137 days in ambient sediments to 4.5 days in sediment chronically exposed to high levels of diesel-contaminated sediments for 28 days. Two- and three-ring PAH, including naphthalenes, phenanthrenes, and dibenzothiophenes constituted the bulk of PAH composition of diesel and were rapidly metabolized Alkylated PAH were also readily metabolized. The rapid removal of PAH suggests that even if the marsh were exposed to chronically high levels of petroleum hydrocarbons, chemical evidence of the contaminants would not be detected in sediments. Collectively, these results are consistent with the hypothesis that the bacterial community in this salt marsh has adapted to chronic exposure to petroleum hydrocarbons.

Student Participation: 1 undergraduate.

Publications:

Carman, K.R., Fleeger, J.W., and S.M. Pomarico. In press. Response of a benthic food web to hydrocarbon contamination. Limnology and Oceanography

Carman, K.R., Fleeger, J.W., Means, J.C., Pomarico, S.M., and McMillin, D.J. 1995. Experimental investigation of the effects of polynuclear aromatic hydrocarbons on an estuarine sediment food web. Marine Environmental Research 40: 289-318.

2.2.7 Bioremediation of Aromatic Heterocycles from Petroleum, Produced Water, and Pyrogenic Sources in Marine Sediments: Transformation Pathway Studies and Evaluation of Remediation Approaches Task 19920

Principal Investigator: James W. Catallo

Status: Completed, final report issued.

MMS Relevance: Bioremediation following contamination of coastal environments by oil spills and permitted discharges holds considerable promise for restoration of natural ecological function following damage. This has been shown in demonstration studies. There is, however, relatively little data on exactly how bioremediation proceeds. This lack of basic understanding limits our ability to anticipate the effects of attempted bioremediation under natural conditions in a variety of habitats. Dr. Catallo's project will provide such basic understanding.

Project Description: The intent of the research is to determine (a) pathways of biodeterioration of pollutants in the estuarine environment, (b) the identities and roles of individual species participating in transformations, and (c) the ecological significance of these changes. Having such information, bioremediation strategies can be optimized. The principal methodology employed will be tracking of biodeterioration in microcosms by indigenous microbes of labeled compounds. There are two tasks. Task I employs deuterated N-, O-, and S- heterocycles and sediments from Terrebonne Bay in aerobic and anaerobic microcosms. The labeled compounds will be extracted from the microcosms and characterized by GC-MS technology. Task II is a experimental manipulation based upon the results of Task I. Employing microbes found active in Task I, an attempt will be made to maximize deterioration of target pollutants through microcosm control of oxygen and bacterial nutrients.

Student Participation: Three undergraduate workers.

Publications:

Junk, T. and W.J. Catallo. 1997. Organic reactions in supercritical polar fluids. Chem Soc. Rev. 26:401-406.

Junk, T., W.J. Catallo, and L.D. Civils.1997. Synthesis of polydeuterated benzothiazoles via supercritical deuteration of anilines. Journal of Labeled Compounds and Radiopharmacy. 38:625-630.

Junk, T., W.J. Catallo, and J. Elguero. 1997. Synthesis in superheated aqueous media: Preparation of fully deuterated pyrazoles and quinoxalines. Tetrhedron Letters 38:6309-6312.

Catallo, W.J. 1997. Effects of Hydrology and Associated Biogeochemical Processes on Transformation and Transport of Aromatic Hydrocarbons and N-, O-, and S-heterocycles in Coastal wetland sediments. Proc. WERC/HSRC Joint Conf. On the Environment pp 161-165.

2.2.8 Bioremediation of Spilled Hydrocarbons Task 19921

Principal Investigators: Paul LaRock, Dr. Vincent Wilson, and Dr. Maud Walsh

Status: Final Report Pending

MMS Relevance: The impact to the environment from an oil spill is not the immediate damage, but any residual damage that remains after attempts are made to repair the damage. Therefore, if MMS is to consider the true cost of development and promote minimization of impacts, the agency must be able to measure the effectiveness of proposed remediation techniques. Seeding spills with oil degrading bacteria or otherwise promoting bacterial degradation of spilled oils is microbial remediation techniques that have been proposed and offered commercially. However, critical evaluation of the effectiveness is hampered by analyses that are too general to provide unequivocal results. Dr. LaRock proposes to combine two technologies to provide the needed specificity. A molecular probe will be developed to assay for a known oil degrading bacteria and chromatographic technology can be used to monitor the consumption of a single molecular component of oil.

Project Description: In oil producing and handling areas, considerable attention revolves around cleanup and containment practices in the event of releases to the environment. Over the decades we have seen an evolution in oil-spill remediation , but unfortunately the conditions under which spills occur and the predominating meteorological or geographical factors often prevent the successful application of any physical cleanup procedure. It is possible, however, to utilize bioremediation procedures to overcome these limitations. In general bioremediation involves either seeding bacteria that have been adapted in the laboratory to rapidly degrade hydrocarbons, or modification of the environment with "fertilizers" to promote the development of natural microbial communities. The principal difference in the two approaches is that fertilizer addition entails a relatively long lag period before the microbes become effective, whereas the seeded bacteria begin the degradation process immediately, but are often displaced by native species.

The effectiveness of bioremediation depends primarily on the prevailing environmental factors and consequently some rapid means of assessing the degradation process is essential in producing optimal results. The usual approaches to quantifying bioremediation efficacy include enumeration of microbial populations, the rate of consumption of oxygen or production of carbon dioxide, and the actual hydrocarbon degradation rate determined from a complete hydrocarbon analysis. Each of these methods has its advantages and disadvantages, but primarily they are either time consuming or nonspecific. However, by using molecular probes that are species-specific for the selected hydrocarbon-utilizing bacteria, and a single, readily quantifiable hydrocarbon ($^{14}0$-hexadecane), it becomes possible to quickly address the questions of bacterial survival, community structure, the efficacy of seeding, and the effects of environmental constraints on biodegradational effectiveness. With such information in hand it is possible to develop a remediation model that would predict, within limits, what parameters would be most important in optimizing the bioremediation program under the prevailing environmental conditions, and which cultures and nutrients would best serve the purpose.

Students, 3 MS: Brent Tatford, Mat Mahler and Lisa Stewart Donovan; 3 Postdocs: Brenda Bennison, Naomi Ward-Rainey and Susan Meiers

Publications:

Wilson, V.L., Tatford, B.C., Yin, X., Rajki, S.C., Walsh, M.M.and LaRock, P. Species-specific detection of hydrocarbon utilizing bacteria. J. Microbiol. Methods, in press.

Donovan, L.S., Meiers, S. and LaRock, P. Competition and displacement of seeded hydrocarbon utilizing bacteria. In preparation.

2.2.9 The Potential for Accelerated Bioremediation and Restoration of Oil-Impacted Marshes Through the Selection of Superior Oil-Tolerant Vegetation Task 19927

Principal Investigators: Mark W. Hester and Irving A Mendelssohn

Status: Completed final report issued.

M. W. Hester, Q. Lin, I. A. Mendelssohn, and D. J. Desroches. 1998. Potential for accelerated bioremediation and restoration of oil-impacted marshes through the selection of superior oil-tolerant vegetation. A final report by Southeastern Louisiana University and Louisiana State University for the U.S. Department of the Interior, Minerals Management Service Gulf of Mexico OCS Region, New Orleans, LA. Contract No. 14-35-0001-30660-19927 OCS Study MMS 2000-042 48 pp.

MMS Relevance: When considering the wisdom of offshore development, MMS must weight the benefits against losses such as environmental impact due to accidental oil spills. However, the final cost of spill impact should not be based upon the acute effects. Remediation technologies are now advancing and hold out promise of repairing damage and reducing final environmental cost. In a marsh-dominated coast, such as the shore of the NW Gulf of Mexico, plants are a structuring element in the habitat. Plant loss is a major cost of spills that could be corrected by remediation. Dr. Hester combines plant physiology and horticulture is an effort to see is petroleum tolerant strains of natural plants can be identified and used in remediation.

Project Summary: The proposed research project addressed the question of whether superior oil-tolerant populations of Spartina patens and Spartina alterniflora can be identified that display: (1) superior growth response and plant production under oil stress, (2) superior vegetative regrowth through oiled sediment, and (3) superior oil degradation potential.

To accomplish these objectives, genetically diverse populations of Spartina patens and S. alterniflora collected from coastal marshes of Louisiana and Texas will be established in a uniform potting mix and oiled with South Louisiana crude oil at rates known to be stressful from our previous research. Measurements of plant growth parameters and physiological response will be made on treatments and controls during the growing season, after which an initial harvest of aboveground biomass will be conducted. Vegetative regrowth through the oiled sediment will be monitored for an additional three months. A final harvest will then be conducted and residual oil in the sediment determined. Populations will analyzed for superior oil tolerance in terms of leaf expansion rates, photosynthesis, live above ground biomass, live-to-dead biomass ratio, vegetative regrowth, and oil degradation potential. Data will be analyzed using univariate and multivariate statistical techniques. Principal components analysis will be utilized to determine if populations possessing a suite of superior oil-tolerant characteristics can be identified.

Of the ten genotypes assessed in both <u>Spartina patens</u> and <u>S</u>. <u>alterniflora</u>, several genotypes in each could be identified that displayed superior oil tolerance in terms of single and multiple plant-growth responses to oiling. This finding has important ecological and applied value. Oil-tolerant genotypes of these species may be planted in marsh rehabilitation (restoration and creation) projects in areas of high oil activity, thereby potentially increasing the resiliency of these marshes to oiling, should an oil spill occur. Of the three oil-tolerant genotypes of <u>Spartina patens</u>, two also displayed the potential for accelerating the degradation of oil indicating the potential for enhanced rates of bioremediation (phytoremediation).

When oiled, these oil-tolerant genotypes characteristically displayed less tissue death, maintained higher plant productivity, and demonstrated a greater ability to successfully produce new shoots through the oiled soil. Analysis of oil-degradation factor scores in S. patens further revealed that two of the three oil-tolerant genotypes demonstrated significantly greater oil-degradation potential than other genotypes. For both species, it is likely that in the long term (and under field conditions), greater rates of oil degradation would be associated with those genotypes that display less stress and greater plant productivity.

Students: Graduate Student Q. Lin, and three undergraduate workers.

Publications:

DesRoches, D. J., G. P. Shaffer, M. W. Hester, and S. Miller. Submitted. A mesocosm approach to determine the suitability of processed drill cuttings for wetland restoration and creation. Ecological Engineering.

Dowty, R. A., G. P. Shaffer, M. W. Hester, G. W. Childers, F. M. Campo, and M. C. Greene. Submitted. Phytoremediation of small-scale oil spills in fresh marsh environments: a mesocosm simulation. Marine Environmental Research.

Hester, M. W., I. A. Mendelssohn. 1999. Long-term recovery of a Louisiana brackish marsh plant community from oil-spill impact: vegetation response and mitigating effects of marsh surface elevation. Marine Environmental Research 49: 1-22.

Pezeshki, R., M. W. Hester, Q. Lin, and J. A. Nyman. 1999. The effects of oil spill and clean-up on dominant US Gulf Coast marsh macrophytes: a review. Environmental Pollution 108: 1-11.

2.2.10 Historical Reconstruction of the Pollutant Loading and Biological Responses in the Central Gulf of Mexico Shelf Sediments Task 19930

Principal Investigators: Eugene Turner, Ed Overton, B. K. Sen Gupta, and N.N. Rabalais

Project Status: Ongoing.

MMS Relevance : In an effort to overcome the difficulty of identifying chronic effects of oil and gas development in the OCS, MMS has placed great emphasis upon analyses of pollutants in sediments. However, the Gulf of Mexico poses several challenges to the interpretation of these results. Whatever the "pollutant signal" of OCS development is, it is only a part of a background of other signals from the entire Mississippi River Basin and more local discharges. Chemical tracers can only be used confidently after this background is known. Dr. Turner and his colleagues will examine this background by constructing a historical time-line of pollutant loading.

Project Summary- A pervasive, continuing, and confounding feature of the OCS Program and continental shelf investigations involves the influences of regional forcing functions, such as riverine discharge and concentrations, climate and exchanges with estuaries that vary 'naturally' and have also changed over decades from landscape-scale influences. These influences complicate estimations of the more localized releases of oil and gas drilling and production operations. Frequent small contaminant releases and large infrequent contaminants releases, are difficult to detect in a dynamic ecosystem under the influence of a large river. In this context, it was proposed to document the changes in chemical contaminants of the central Gulf of Mexico continental shelf sediments, the biogeochemical signature of ecosystem changes found within them, and the biological response in the foraminiferal community.

The approach is to use dated sediment cores as part of an ongoing and integrated project under the Louisiana Sea Grant Program (estuarine) and the NOAA NECOP Program (continental shelf). The work requires: (1) careful collection of sediment cores from the continental shelf, (2) dating these cores in approximately 5 year increments, (3) determination of sediment N, P and organic C, and trace metals and organic compounds, including petroleum biomarkers (e.g., Zn, Pb, Cd, Ba, alkyl PAH, triterpenes, sterenes), within core segments, and (4) quantitative estimation of benthic foraminiferal species abundance (a) in surface sediments to assess the effects of hydrocarbon contamination on these shelled protozoans (because of toxicity or oxygen depletion), and, (b) in downcore sediments to interpret environmental changes in historical time (some possibly related to hydrocarbon contamination), but in addition to regional changes and natural variability.

The questions addressed include: What are the historical changes in contaminant storage of the Outer Continental Shelf (OCS) ecosystem? Are the anticipated biomarkers of petroleum sources localized or regional; are they temporally isolated in the sediment core? To what depth contour and distance downstream of the Mississippi River plume does the oilfield or regional (Mississippi River) framework extend? How does the contaminant storage near or around oilfields contribute to the regional framework influenced by the Mississippi River discharge plume? Are these changes reflected in the assemblages of benthic foraminifera and other ecosystem indicators?

Student Participation: Graduate Emile Platon Ph.D and P.J. Perry Ph.D

Publications: None yet.

2.2.11 Studying and Verifying the Use of Chemical Biomarkers for Identifying and Quantitating Oil Residues in the Environment Task 19933

Principal Investigator: Edward B. Overton and Charles B. Henry, Jr.

Status: Completed, final report issued.

MMS Relevance: In the complex mix of pollution that may be linked to OCS development is an analytical problem: most analytical methods provide little or no discrimination between source and concentration values generated. The data are blindly accepted as real. When studying oil pollution in the marine environment, the analytical approach must be able to differentiate sources of contamination and quantify oil residues in complex environmental samples. This project seeks to develop that quantification.

Project Description: Advances in analytical chemistry have improved our ability to fingerprint and track the fate of spilled oil. As our ability to assess trace level oil pollution improves, matrix affects and multiple pollution sources complicate our attempts. New approaches such as hopane-normalization and self-normalizing fingerprint indexes have been proposed and utilized to some degree, but further validation is required. Source identification or source fingerprinting as it is commonly called, is based on the use of high-resolution gas chromatography/mass spectrometry (GC/MS) analyses of selected components in oil and its residues. Quantifying oil and oily residues can be obtained from two methods. First, quantities of oil and oily residues can be directly measured as "Total petroleum hydrocarbons" using appropriate analytical methods. Because of the heterogeneous distribution of oil in aqueous systems, this method requires extensive replication before statistically valid results can be achieved. Second, oil quantities can be inferred by examining the distribution of selected hydrocarbon components remaining in the oily residues found in the environment. This method is based on the fact that not all components in oil are readily degraded by natural weathering process. Therefore, if we compare the quantity of hydrocarbons remaining relative to the quantity of undegraded components, we can estimate the percent of residual oil remaining after environmental weathering. This latter method is known as biomarker normalization. While biomarker normalization shows great promise as a tool for both identifying spilled oil and quantifying environmental residues, it is not a perfect one and can, in contaminated systems, overestimate the actual percent degradation. A goal of this study is to refine the use of biomarkers as tools for oil spill identification and assessment and to verify the "State of the art" approach with both laboratory and field evaluation studies. An extensive literature review has been completed and, as a possible product from this evaluation, a manual to aid researchers in developing analytical chemistry approaches to investigate oil pollution in the marine environment is being generated.

Student Participation: One under grad, one graduate.

Publications: None yet.

2.2.12 How Does Produced Water Cause a Reduction in the Genetic Diversity of Harpacticoid Copepods? Task 19949

Principal Investigators: John W. Fleeger and David W. Foltz

Status: Ongoing.

MMS Relevance: The general public sometimes objects to offshore oil and gas development for a variety of reasons. Among these is a persistent belief that such development causes major environmental damage. In keeping with its obligation to manage OCS resources wisely MMS has supported numerous studies intended to find such impacts. While all these studies are subject to technical criticism, the results support the conclusion that impacts to fauna are restricted to the vicinity of the development, and more widely spread chronic impacts, if they exist, are lost in the statistical noise of natural and other manmade changes.

Project Description: An important finding of the GOOMEX project was that benthic harpacticoid copepods in the proximity of development sites had reduced genetic heterogeneity. This result, based on mitochondrial DNA, were interpreted as an example of a chronic impact at the population level. Due to the fact that such chronic impacts are seldom documented, this is an important finding that requires investigation and verification. In order to eliminate the multiple uncontrolled factors inherent in field studies, this project will be based on laboratory experimentation. It will employ lab cultured hapacticoid copepods in the species or species complex *Cletocampus deitersi*. Two hypotheses will be tested. First, that metal contaminants surrounding long-term production sites are capable of reducing genetic diversity. Second, that natural populations contain cryptic (unrecognized) species with sufficient genetic difference to confuse field results. Genetic diversity will be quantified by means of polymerase chain reaction, restriction fragment length polymorphism, and direct sequencing.

Given the inability of traditional population survey methods to detect chronic impacts, the finding in GOOMEX that harpacticoid copepod populations near platforms apparently differ from those remote from the platform requires verification. The primary nature of the apparent impact was that harpacticoids, an abundant component of the smaller benthic fauna, had reduced genetic diversity near production sites. The use of genetic information in environmental studies is in its infancy and several factors other than oil and gas related impact might be a factor. If the Montagna results are confirmed, then a new tool for impact studies may have been found. If the Montagna results are not confirmed, this study may allow for the confounding effects to be identified.

The finding that harpacticoid copepods near long-term production sites have reduced genetic diversity is especially important. It reports an apparent, rarely documented, effect upon a population, and it employs genetic testing not previously applied to oil and gas effect studies in the Gulf of Mexico. It is important that this finding be investigated in an experimental mode to refute, confirm, or better understand the result.

In this study two aspects of the GOOMEX results will be carefully examined. The first is a test of the conclusion that apparent reduction in genetic diversity is actually caused the hydrocarbon and metal contamination near platforms. This critical causal link could not be established by the field sampling of the GOOMEX project. The second part of the project will examine the possibility that the Street/Montagna results simply reflect the variable distribution of cryptic species. In this study cryptic species are considered distinct species which have escaped recognition by traditional morphological examination but can be recognized by molecular genetics.

Two formal null hypotheses will be tested:

1. Exposure of lab populations of *Cletocampus deitersi* to polyaromatic hydrocarbons and metals in oil well effluent for three generations causes no reduction in genetic diversity.

26

2. The existence of a gradient of contamination has no influence upon the number of cryptic species within the *Cletocampus deitersi* group.

The feasibility of this project is due to the special expertise of the collaborating labs of Drs. Fleeger and Foltz. Toxicity assays on meiofauna cultures and microcosms is a specialty of the Fleeger lab, where assays of the effects of polyaromatic hydrocarbons have been extremely successful. Inclusion of metal effects, as required by the findings of the GOOMEX project. Determination of molecular genetic identity and heterogeneity is the specialty of the Foltz lab.

The effect of contaminants on genetic diversity will consist of two phases. Preliminary work will develop a exposure methodology. Once that has been completed a factorial design will be used to assay effects on *Cletocampus deitersi* collected in uncontaminated areas. Field-collected copepods will be exposed to contaminants for three generations. At the end of each generation individuals will be harvested for analysis of two mitochondrial DNA gene regions. The experimental design is intended to test for independent and combined effects of polyaromatic hydrocarbons and metals. A finding of reduced genetic diversity would confirm the Street/Montagna findings.

The possibility that the GOOMEX results simply reflect species distributions will be tested in the field along a well-established contamination gradient near Port Fourchon, La. Specimens will be collected from this gradient and subjected to genetic analysis to determine if there is a shift in the population at the species level.

Students: 3 undergraduates, Post Doc: Axayacatl Rocha-Olivares

Publications: None yet.

2.2.13 Long-term Effects of Contaminants from OCS Produced Waters Discharges Task 19937

Principal Investigators: Ed Overton and Nancy Rabalais

Status: Completed, report issued.

Rabalais, N.N, L.E. Smith, C.B. Henry, Jr., P.O. Roberts, E. Overton. 1998. Long-term Effects of Contaminants from OCS Produced Waters Discharges at Pelican Island facility, Louisiana. OCS Study MMS 98-0039. U.S. Department of Interior, Minerals Management Service, Gulf of Mexico OCS Region, New Orlean, LA. 88pp.

MMS Relevance: To a certain extent MMS's regulatory mission in the Gulf of Mexico was initiated after the fact, long after oil and gas operations had begun. Therefore, before and after studies, the strongest scientific approach to impact, are seldom possible. However, it is possible to gain some understanding of the impacts actually caused by "during-and-after" studies that track the course of recovery when an impacting activity has stopped. This study by Rabalais and Overton is precisely that. It is a 9th year examination of an inshore produced waters discharge facility that was previously characterized at it cessation of operation in 1987, two years later in 1989. This study repeated the characterization in 1996.

Project Summary: There are over 1,200 produced water discharge sites in coastal Louisiana and Texas that after cessation of discharge may continue to have impacts on sediment and water quality. During a previous MMS-funded study, Rabalais documented at the Pelican Island, La. facility:

1. the presence of high concentrations of produced water derived hydrocarbons,

2. long-term accumulation of contaminants and their resistance to degradation,

3. persistence of produced water origin hydrocarbons adjacent to an abandoned produced water facility, and

4. persistent effects of residual produced water contaminants on the benthic infauna adjacent to an abandoned produced water facility. These results indicate that a legacy of impacts may remain within coastal environment after the cessation of OCS oil and gas production activities. We propose a preliminary project to document potential long-term impacts of residual contaminants.

Hydrocarbon contamination was found to be less than at 2 years post operation, but persisted deeper in cores. There was evidence that additional contamination from unknown sources had occurred since 1989. Benthic fauna showed place-to-place differences, but these did not appear to be closely linked to contamination as had been found in 87 and 89.

Student Participation: Paulene O. Roberts, Ms Student, 1 undergraduate student worker.

Publications: None yet.

2.3   Research Area: Offshore Structure Ecology

Six projects have been funded in the area of offshore structure ecology at a cost to MMS of $2,807,000 and equal match largely provided in-kind by participating platform operators. The nucleus of these studies have been hydroacoustic and ROV surveys of fish fauna (tasks 19915 and 19947) which developed the working relations with the platform operators. Taking advantage of this opportunity an additional project has looked at larval fish and zooplankton (task 19926 extended as 19961), and another project has looked at the attached biota (19932). In a class of its own as a project with considerable public following is a very active trans-Gulf bird migration study (task 19938).

2.3.1   Spatial and Seasonal Variation in the Biomass and Size Distribution of Fishes Associated with Oil and Gas Platforms in the Northern Gulf of Mexico Task 19915

Principal Investigators: David R. Stanley and Charles A. Wilson

Status: Completed, final report issued.

Stanley, D.R. and C.A. Wilson. 2000. Seasonal and spatial variation in the biomass and size frequency distribution of fish associated with oil and gas platforms in the northern Gulf of Mexico. A final report for the U.S. Department of the Interior, Minerals Management Service Gulf of Mexico OCS Region, New Orleans, LA. OCS Study MMS 2000-005.

MMS Relevance - Recreational and commercial fishing at offshore structures has become an important integral part of coastal resource utilization in all Gulf of Mexico OCS States. Therefore MMS must consider the consequences of impacts upon these resource users when decisions are made concerning the establishment of new structures and the removal of old. A key unresolved question about offshore structures is whether they simply attract fish or contribute to the actual production of fish stocks. If they only attract, then structures pose a threat of over exploitation as fishermen target the fish at easily located places of congregation. If they contribute to production, then structures cause a positive addition to the resource being exploited. MMS needs to know which is the case. LSU has made a substantial investment in acoustical and ROV technology in order to develop appropriate means of surveying fish populations at structures. This CMI project allows for application of this newer technology to MMS' question. This project is in partnership with Mobile USA.

Project Summary: Complimentary sampling methods of visual surveys and quantitative dual beam hydroacoustic surveys were used to document the assemblage of fishes associated with three petroleum platforms in the northern Gulf of Mexico. With the sampling protocol established, the objectives of this research were to use dual beam hydroacoustics in conjunction with visual point count surveys to measure the density and size distribution of fishes associated with three petroleum platforms off the Louisiana coast. The goals of this research were to determine the effect of water depth on fish density, size distribution and species composition and ultimately to measure the fisheries value of platforms of different depths in the same geographical region.

At the shallowest site, South Timbalier 54 the decline in fish density with distance from the platform was precipitous; beyond 18 m fish densities were similar to that of the open waters of the northern Gulf of Mexico. At the deeper sites a drop in fish density with distance from the site existed, although fish density was much higher to greater distances. At both Grand Isle 94 (GI94, water depth 60 m) and Green Canyon 18 (GC18, water depth 219 m) fish density approached that found in the open waters of the Gulf of Mexico after a distance of approximately 50 m. Six species made up over 90 percent of the fishes observed at each site on any survey and platform assemblages could be characterized as not specious and dominated by a few individual species. By site the dominant six species (highest to lowest abundance) were; GC18; creolefish, blue runner, Bermuda chub, almaco jack, amberjack, and barracuda; GI94; blue runner, horseeye jack, red snapper, mangrove snapper, gray triggerfish and barracuda; ST54; Atlantic spadefish, bluefish, blue runner, mangrove snapper, red snapper and sheepshead. While the species found at each site were somewhat unique and the dominant species at each site was different, a large amount of overlap of observed species existed between sites, especially adjacent sites. Seasonal migrations were common at each of the study sites. Common seasonal migrations observed in the winter were the appearance of Florida pompano and bluefish at ST54; and the appearance of blue runner and barracuda at GI94 and GC18. Summer seasonal observations included the appearance o tarpon and cobia at ST54, an increase in abundance of cobia, red snapper, greater amberjack and almaco jack at GI94, while no summer migrants were observed at GC18.

The results of this project demonstrate the variability in abundance, size and species composition of fishes associated with petroleum platforms. Similar results from earlier studies have been found with natural and artificial reefs. The variability in density and the size distribution of fishes at petroleum platforms in this project was linked to temporal, spatial and environmental variables.

This research confirms the variability of fish assemblages associated with petroleum platforms and reinforces the need to sample on each side and throughout the water column to obtain an accurate estimate of fish abundance. The high abundance of fishes found at the sites demonstrates the importance of petroleum platforms to the marine environment of the northern GOM. Although some variance was observed, 10,000 to 30,000 fishes were found per site at any one time and since over 1,000 platforms are located in similar water depths it is clear that these structures impact the fisheries of the region.

Student Participation: One Ph.D. student James Tolan, and 3 undergraduate students.

Publications:

Stanley, D.R., and C.A. Wilson. In press. Variation in the density and species composition of fishes associated with three petroleum platforms as measured with dual beam hydroacoustics. Proceedings 1997 AFS Acoustic Symposium, American Fisheries Society, Monterey CA. Fisheries Science.

Stanley, D.R., and C.A. Wilson. 1999. Spatial variation in fish density at three petroleum platforms as measured with dual-beam hydroacoustics in the northern Gulf of Mexico. Proceedings 1997 AFS Artificial Reef Symposium, American Fisheries Society, Monterey CA. Gulf Science.

Stanley, D.R., and C.A. Wilson. 1996. The use of hydroacoustics to determine abundance and size distribution of fishes associated with a petroleum platform. International Council on the Exploration of the Sea, Journal of Marine Science. 53:473-475.

2.3.2 Effect of Depth and Location on the Composition and Abundance of Nektonic Fishes Associated with Petroleum Platforms in the Gulf of Mexico Task 19947

Principal Investigators: David Stanley and Charles Wilson

Status: Ongoing.

MMS Relevance: Previous hydroacoustic surveys at three platforms have established a reliable methodology for fish assemblage surveying. The full utility of such data requires studies that confirm their geographic applicability. This study makes that extension.

Project Description: This is an extension of the previous study and examines five platforms situated East and West of the Mississippi River mouth at depths between 33 and 150m. The same hydroacoustic and ROV techniques employed in task 19915 were used.

Student Participation: M.S. student Aaron Pierce and one undergraduate.

Publications: As listed for related task 19915.

2.3.3 The Post-Larval and Juvenile Fish Nursery Ground/Refugia Function of Offshore Oil and Gas Platforms Task 19926 & Offshore Petroleum

Platforms: Functional Significance for Larval Fish Across Longitudinal and Latitudinal Gradients Task 19961

Principal Investigator: Richard F. Shaw and Mark Benfield

Status: Initial task 19926 extended as 19961 and ongoing.

MMS Relevance - Recreational and commercial fishing at offshore structures has become an important integral part of coastal resource utilization in all Gulf of Mexico OCS States. Therefore MMS must consider the consequences of impacts upon these resource users when decisions are made concerning the establishment of new structures and the removal of old. One intriguing possibility is that offshore structures are actually serving as nursery grounds for larval fish. If this can be demonstrated it will be definitive evidence that structures add to fish stocks. The use of larval light traps in a new way of examining this important question.

Project Summary: Our proposed research has four specific objectives. (1) Provide information on the role oil and gas platforms play as important nursery grounds or refugia for postlarval and juvenile fish, which could thereby contribute to and enhance overall fish production. (2) Supplement, compare, and test a relatively new sampling technique, light trap methodology (which is capable of sampling large numbers of late stage postlarval and juvenile fishes in structurally complex environments) with traditional sampling techniques (i.e. plankton net collections). (3) Respond to specific fisheries management requests for basic biological information on reef fish, e.g., larval, postlarval and juvenile taxonomy, seasonality, vertical distribution, relative abundance, and possibly otolith daily ring validation and age/growth estimation. (4) To extend the geographic range of the above three results.

If we are to begin to address the yet-unresolved, fundamental question of whether offshore rigs simply attract/concentrate fish or indirectly enhance production (increase biomass increase spawning or nursery ground habitat, growth, survivorship of young, etc.), we must begin to document the habitat function of rigs and the species which utilize this unique habitat; to assess the role that rigs play in influencing the distribution and abundance of young fishes; and to address rigs as nursery grounds or refugia for postlarval and juvenile fishes associated with hard bottom habitat (i.e., Are rigs areas of higher abundance than background water column densities as estimated by the State-Federal Southeastern Area Monitoring and Assessment Program (SEAMAP) or MMS-LATEX surveys utilizing plankton net collections? What is the larval, postlarval and juvenile seasonality, relative abundance (based on light trap catch per unit effort), distribution (vertical and across shelf), and growth rate of fish associated with rigs? Specifically, over a three-year period, we will investigate whether there is a substantial temporal (daily or lunar) or spatial (sampling at 20m, 61m and 229m depth platforms) nursery ground/refugia function to rig structure as determined by statistically-designed collections of reef and pelagic finfish species showing consistent affinity for platform architecture, i.e., Do rigs have a fisheries production component? We hypothesize that catch rates, densities or species composition are greater and more diverse than background (non-platform) conditions determined from historical data from oceanographic cruises. Consequently, we propose the first directed study addressing this basic question of platform fisheries production of early life history stages (i.e., it is the first systematic determination of baseline data on the larval, postlarval and juvenile fish community within the vertical structure of rigs).

Students: Ph.D.,James Ditty and Frank Hernadez, five undergraduate employees. Post Doctoral study Dr. Mark Benfield was given faculty rank during the project.

Publications: None yet.

2.3.4 Characterization of Algal-Invertebrate Mats at CMI Study Platforms Task 19932

Principal Investigators: Robert Carney and Russell Chapman

Status started in cycle, final report in preparation

MMS Relevance: With thousands of offshore structures in the northwest Gulf of Mexico, artificial substrate communities have probably become part of the ecological fabric of the region. While the consequences about rig removal have focused on the economically important fish species, full understanding of the impact must also include knowledge about the algal-invertebrate mats that encrust these structures. This project is intended as a trial effort at cost-effective ecological studies of that system, taking advantage of the three platforms available to CMI investigators.

Project Summary: The project was designed as a two-year time-series examination of platform fouling communities at three CMI sites. The intent was to identify the most effective means of survey and to identify the most relevant ecological questions. SCUBA diving from working platforms proved highly problematic due to weather and operational disruptions. Never the less, a sufficient portion of the design was completed. For sessile fauna, the offshore trends resembled those previously reported. For mobile fauna, however, the results suggested a dual foodweb system. While sessile filter feeders depend upon phytoplankton/detritus flux, extremely abundant amphipods, polychaetes, and juvenile ophiuroids seem to be dependent upon an in-situ film of algae and bacteria. It was speculated that these algal grazers might represent a greater export to the surrounding ecosystem than the sessile population.

Student Participation: Undergraduates 4, Ph.D. James Tolan, and Post-doctoral Shaughnassey.

Publications: None yet.

2.3.5 Comparison of Organisms at Two Artificial Reefs Task 19960

Principal Investigator David Stanley, Charles Wilson, Richard Shaw, and Quenton Dokken

Status: Ongoing

MMS Relevance: Related CMI projects have produced information on platform fish assemblages that are applicable to issues of platform removal and artificial reef creation. These results, however, are based upon a very small platform structure and geographic sample (three platforms off Louisiana) and may lack broader applicability. This project seeks to determine the breadth of application by examining fish fauna on platforms and artificial reefs off both Texas and Louisiana.

Project Description: Three structure systems will be examined: a toppled artificial reef (West Cameron 616/617), a partially removed platform (High Island 355), and a production platform (West Cameron 618). Data includes hydroacoustic estimates of area of influence, fish density, fish size distributions, visual survey, light trap sampling, hook and line, and water column physics and chemistry.

Student Participation: Two master's students Aaron Pierce and Kris Karlsson.

Publications: None yet.

2.3.6 Interactions Between Migrating Birds and Offshore Oil and Gas Structures off the Louisiana Coast Task 19938

Principal: James Van Remsen, Robert W. Russell, Sidney A. Gauthreaux, Clemsen University

Status: Ongoing, Dr. Remsen has been replaced by Dr. Russell as PI.

MMS Relevance: Migratory bird species in eastern North America are experiencing long-term population declines. Of the many explanations for this decline is disruption of successful migration. Since the numerous OCS structures in the Gulf of Mexico lie under migration paths, it is important to know what types of structure-bird interactions take place. With such knowledge it may be possible to minimize impacts and even enhance migration success.

Project Description: Direct observation is made of bird use of platforms (8 week censuses at 5 platforms in spring and winter). A larger-scale overview is developed from analysis of radar intensity data. Salvaged dead specimens are being cryogenically stored at LSU to support necropsies.

Student Participation: Post Doc Robert W. Russell, Daniel G. Christian (Ph.D)

Publications: None yet.

2.4 Research Area: Physical Oceanography and Meteorology Component

Twelve projects have been funded in the area of physical oceanography and meteorology at a cost to MMS of $2,661,000 and equal match from LSU. A total of sixteen task numbers were assigned due to the manner in which continuations were handled. Two (combined tasks 19912 and 19925) addressed air quality effects of OCS discharges. One (combined tasks 19917, 19953 and 19965) is a progressively more comprehensive modeling of shallow-water circulation and its influence on the estuarine ecosystem. Two (tasks 19908 and 19952) applied the most advanced 3D-circulation model to the entire Gulf of Mexico with excellent results. Five (Tasks 19936, 19942, 19943, 19948, and 19928) have addressed shelf coastal currents depending heavily on data and hypotheses generated during the LATEX study. One is addressing wave climate modeling (task 19911 as amended) and one has deployed pressure meters and CTD arrays off Louisiana (task 19922).

2.4.1 A Numerical Modeling Study of the Gulf of Mexico under Present and Past Environmental Conditions Task 19908

Principal Investigator: Masamichi Inoue

Status: Final report issued:

Inoue, M. and S. E. Welsh. 1996. Numerical simulation of Gulf of Mexico circulation under present and glacial climatic conditions. OCS Study MMS 96-0067. U. S. Dept. of the Interior, Minerals Management Service, Gulf of Mexico OCS Region, New Orleans, La. 146 pp.

MMS Relevance: The fact that the continental slope in the northern Gulf of Mexico is part of a massive delta system has profound consequences for oil and gas exploitation which are not encountered on more typical, non-deltaic, slopes. One suite of these consequences has to do with the effect of ancient sea levels on deltaic deposition. In effect, the continental slope of the northern Gulf is still undergoing adjustments to the transition from Wisconsinan to Modern conditions. Any correct and useful synthesis of slope stability information for this region must understand the past environments. The dissertation project of Susan Welsh supported by this CMI is an innovative look at the past. Through a paleo-circulation model, MMS gains both a better understanding of the whole Gulf circulation, and an past geological regimes.

Project Description: A three dimensional circulation model was developed from Pacanaowski's Modular Ocean Model. Special treatment was required for simulation of flow through the straits of Yucatan and Florida. An artificial feedback between the outflow through the Straits of Florida and inflow through Yucatan was programmed into the model. This prevented open boundaries in the model and eliminated the need to model a larger portion of the Atlantic. In spite of this artificiality, realistic inflow conditions were assured by forcing the flow crossing the 82.375° W line of latitude to have the observed flow and shear of the Caribbean Current. West of this region of imposed conditions, flow adjusts to simulated bottom and wind conditions.

The 360m depth range of the Gulf was divided into 15 layers. Four upper layers were 75m thick and eleven lower layers 300m.p bathymetry was derived from the ETOPO5 database with interpolation to 1/8° and smoothing.

Student Participation: Graduate Student: Susan E, Welsh Ph.D

Publications:

Welsh, S. E. and M. Inoue. 1994. A numerical modeling study of the Gulf of Mexico under present environmental, conditions. American Geophysical Union 1994 Fall Meeting. San Francisco, CA.

Welsh, S. E. 1996. A numerical modeling study of the Gulf of Mexico under present and past environmental conditions. Ph.D. Dissertation. Department of Geology & Geophysics, Louisiana State University, Baton Rouge, LA, 206 pp.

2.4.2 A Modeling Study of Gulf of Mexico Deep Water Circulation, Ventilation, and Transport Task 19952

Principal Investigators: Susan E. Welsh and Masamichi Inoue

Status: Completed, final report pending.

MMS Relevance: As the oil and gas industry moves beyond the shelf edge it is increasingly important that the circulation of the entire Gulf of Mexico be understood in three dimensions rather than just near the surface and on the shelf. This project will provide such an overview with special focus upon those processes ventilating deep water. State-of-the-art computer simulation provides a very cost-effective means of obtaining this overview.

Project Description: In this three-year project a numerical circulation model will be used to study the circulation, ventilation and transports of the deep water of the Gulf of Mexico. The objective of this study is to provide: (1) a detailed description of the deep circulation of the Gulf, which appears to be dominated by cyclones associated with the Loop Current (LC) rings; (2) an examination of transport, mixing and ventilation processes in the deep water using Lagrangian techniques; and (3) an estimate of the residence time of deep water in the Gulf using Lagrangian techniques. As offshore oil and gas exploration and production move beyond shelf break and into slope region, detailed knowledge of the deepwater environment is increasingly becoming essential for reasons of design, installation, and safe operation of offshore platforms. Special emphasis will be placed on the slope environment and shelf-slope exchange processes in the northern and western Gulf, which is not only the predominant region for rings to interact with the bathymetry and eventually decay.

The latest version of the Modular Ocean Model version 2 is being implemented with fine horizontal and vertical resolution to adequately resolve mesoscale eddies and the role of bottom bathymetry in the deep circulation. Enhanced vertical resolution on the shelf, quasi-synoptic wind stress, a free surface, and fresh water input from the major rivers will allow for accurate simulation of the Texas-Louisiana shelf circulation, which is important for shelf- slope exchanges. A seasonal variation in the sea-surface temperature, salinity and wind stress, and the seasonal variation in the volume transport and vertical shear of the inflow will also be implemented for realistic simulation of general circulation as well as LC and ring behavior.

Student Participation: Shobarani Tatineni

Publications: None yet.

2.4.3 Wave Climate Modeling and Evaluation Relative to Sand Mining on Ship Shoal, Offshore Louisiana Task 19911

Principal Investigator: Gregory Stone

Status: Completed, final report issued.

MMS Relevance: Recently there has been significant interest in the potential use of clean quartz sand comprising Ship Shoal off the Louisiana coast, as a source for beach replenishment along the rapidly eroding Isles Dernieres barrier system. Preliminary work contracted by the U.S. Minerals Management Service demonstrated that such an undertaking is both technically and economically feasible. It is highly probable that Ship Shoal mitigates the wave climate along the Isles Dernieres, although the degree to which has not been established. Therefore, large-scale extraction of sediment from Ship Shoal should not be attempted prior to a detailed evaluation of the wave and current field in this area. The project is a detailed, quantitative investigation of the impacts associated with dredging material from Ship Shoal for placement along the Isles Dernieres.

Project Description: The project takes a three-fold approach including: (1) Prototype measurement of the wave and current field; (2) mathematical modeling of wave-energy transformation and decay across the inner shelf, and (3) development of a physical model of Ship Shoal in a three dimensional flume at Louisiana State University. It is now well established that barrier islands comprising Isles Dernieres, have been experiencing the highest rates of shoreline retreat in the United States. Historical erosion rates along the Isles Dernieres ranged from 4.8 m/yr. (East Island) to 22.9 m/yr. (Wine Island) over the last century or so. Based on these data, it is estimated that several of the islands will disappear within the next decade or two.

Student Involvement: graduate student: Xiongping Zhang, Ph.D

Publications:

Pepper, D.A., Stone, G.W. and P. Wang. 1998. Wave, current, and sediment interactions on the Louisiana shoreface adjacent to the Isles Derniers. Recent Research in Coastal Louisiana: Conference Proceedings.

Pepper, D.A., G.W. Stone, and P. Wang. 1999. Bottom Boundary Layer Parameters and Sediment Transport on the Louisiana Inner-Shelf During Cold Front Passages. Transactions of the Gulf Coast Association Geological Societies, 49: 432-439.

2.4.4 Measurements of Air Quality and Meteorological Parameters on Breton and Dauphin Islands in the Northeast Gulf of Mexico Task 19912

Principal Investigator, S.A. Hsu

Status: Task completed and extended as a separate task; see 19925 below. A final report has submitted and issued. The final report for task 19925 is, however, more comprehensive.

Hsu, S.A. 1995. Measurements of SO_2 concentrations and atmospheric structure in Delta and Breton Sound Wildlife Refuges. OCS Study MMS 95-0019. U.S. Dept. of the Interior, Minerals Management Service, Gulf of Mexico OCS Region, New Orleans, La. 74pp.

Hsu, S. A. 1996. Analysis of ambient pollutant concentrations and meteorological conditions affecting EPA Class I and II areas in southeastern Louisiana, Volume I: Technical Report. OCS Study MMS 96-0062. U.S. Dept. Of the Interior, Minerals Management Service, Gulf of Mexico OCS Region, New Orleans, Louisiana. 156 pp.

Hsu, S. A. 1996. Analysis of ambient pollutant concentrations and meteorological conditions affecting EPA Class I and II areas in southeastern Louisiana, Volume II: Appendices. OCS Study MMS 96-0063.

MMS Relevance: With increased urbanization and industrialization the Gulf Coast is subject to decreased air quality. Due to the high density of offshore facilities, one component of declining air quality may come from that source. This project is a trial monitoring effort to measure SO2 and NO2 at two wildlife areas.

Project Description: Monitoring stations for the measurement of SO2 and NO2 were established at Breton Sound and Dauphine Island. Additional stations were added via task amendments. See 19925 below.

Student Participation: none

Publications: See 19925 below.

2.4.5 Air Quality and Dispersion Meteorology Over the Northeast Gulf of Mexico: Measurements, Analysis, and Synthesis Task 19925

Principal Investigator: S.A. Hsu

Status: Completed. Comprehensive report covering work under task 19912 and 19925 submitted and issued.

Hsu, S.A. and B.W. Blanchard. 1998. Long-term measurements of SO2 and NO2 concentrations and related meteorological conditions in the northeastern Gulf of Mexico region. OCS Study MMS 98-0020. US Department of the Interior, Minerals Management Service, Gulf of Mexico OCS Region, New Orleans, LA. 308pp.

This report covers data collected 1993-1994

Hsu, S.A. and B.W. Blanchard. Submitted. Air Quality and Dispersion Meteorology Over the Northeast Gulf of Mexico: Measurements, Analyses, and Syntheses. US Dept. of the Interior, Minerals Management Service, Gulf of Mexico OCS Region, New Orleans. LA 184pp.

This study covers data collected 1996-1997.

MMS Relevance: Offshore oil and gas platforms are, in effect, factories which discharge materials into the air and water. Due to the very high concentration of platforms in the Gulf there is a real likelihood that offshore discharges will have a negative impact on coastal air quality. This project examines that possibility.

Project Description: Owing to energy productions from oil platforms in the Gulf of Mexico, it is unavoidable that sulfur compounds such as SO_2, H_2S, and H_2SO_4 are affecting nearby coastal areas. On the other hand, the most recent Clear Air Act does not allow National Seashores and Wildlife Refuges to be polluted. In the offshore region east of the Mississippi River, for example, there are very active areas of energy production and therefore many potential sources for the emissions of SO2 and other sulfur compounds. Unfortunately, downwind from these emission facilities are the Gulf Islands National Seashore and Breton and Delta National Wildlife Refuges.

The objectives of this proposed project are (1) to understand the overwater characteristics of $S0_2$ in this offshore region; (2) to conduct field experiments to measure both $S0_2$ concentration and marine meteorological processes affecting these transports; and (3) to validate or revise existing over-water dispersion models.

This proposed project requires a two-year study. In the summer of 1994 three fluorescent 502 analyzers will be deployed at Breton and Delta National Wildlife Refuges. In addition, upper-air soundings will be conducted near the mouth of the Mississippi River during prevailing SE airflow conditions in the summer. Data from the National Data Buoy Center buoy in the study area will be collected in conjunction with the upper-air data from the National Weather Service at Slidell, Louisiana. The $S0_2$ emission rate and related data are available at the MMS in New Orleans. In 1995, computer models related to 302 dispersion from EPA as well as others such as the U.S. Air Force via Mr. Bill Steorts of MMS at New Orleans will be acquired. In addition, the field data gathered in 1993 and 1994 will be analyzed in order to validate the existing 502 dispersion models. If the model does not agree with the field data, revision of the model may be necessary.

As Stated above, this kind of experiment must be conducted eventually because of the dilemma between energy production and the protection of National Seashores and Wildlife Refuges. It is hoped that this study will determine to what extent the S02 concentration imposes on these "National" environments. Furthermore, the model to be validated or revised will be useful for other coastal regions such as California and Alaska as well as other regions of the Gulf of Mexico.

Two short-term pilot studies were conducted in 93 and 94 in the Breton Sound area. Ambient SO2 and NO2 were less than 5ppb. Concentrations were transport related and maximum with east-northeast winds. Subsequently, Dauphine Island was monitored. It had higher SO2 and similar NO2. Again, concentrations were transport related and did not show strong seasonal influences.

Student Participation: Melvin Francis Martin, Murtuza Jabir Balasinori, and Mansoor
              Sajjad.

Publications: Six reported.

2.4.6 A Pressure Gauge and Moored CTD Array Along the Louisiana Coastal Current Task 19922

Principal Investigator: Steve Murray and Nan Walker

Status: Completed report pending (transferred to Dr. Walker alone upon Dr, Murray's
       retirement from LSU)

MMS Relevance: The arrays deployed provide MMS with increased spatial and temporal resolution to study coastal current dynamics.

Project Description: The objective of the project is to deploy a network of pressure gauges to obtain a synoptic long tome series measurements of the long-shore pressure gradients along the Louisiana Coastal Current from the Mississippi delta westward to the Sabine pass area. Field measurements were made between July 1994 and Jan 1998.

Student Involvement: Eva Jarosz master's student

Publications: None yet.

2.4.7 Analysis and Synthesis of Coastal Boundary Layer Data Task 19936

Principal Investigators: William J. Wiseman, Stephen P. Murray, and Carole Current

Status: Ongoing, transferred to Dr. Rouse upon Dr. Murray's retirement and Dr. Currents' employment by MMS).

MMS Relevancy: The data produce by the LATEX, an openly bid physical oceanography program, exceeded the analytical capability and time restrictions of that study. This CMI project is a cost-effective means of carrying out the needed analyses and gaining understanding of the coastal current. The analysis of LATEX CTD and mooring data and collateral altimetric information falls within the CMI framework area of analyses and synthesis of existing data/information from previous studies. The understanding and quantification of geostrophic flow and related transport across the continental slope is of fundamental value to a broad variety of CMI interests, and the results of this study can be applied to concerns ranging from transport of pollutants and oil spills onto and off of the Louisiana-Texas continental shelf to the direct economic effects of larval distribution in this region, and to the ecological impact of upwelling and movement of water masses onto and off of the continental shelf.

Project Description: Estimation of time-dependent geostrophic transport across the shelf break onto or off of the Louisiana-Texas shelf, and its relation to along-shelf location, is crucial to the understanding of cross-shelf larval migration, upwelling, and transport of pollutants as well as nutrients onto and off of the shelf. The Louisiana-Texas Shelf Physical Oceanography Program (LATEX) has collected a large quantity of mooring and hydrographic data over the Louisiana-Texas continental shelf during the 32 month LATEX field observation period, including hydrographic and mooring data along the 200m isobath.

The proposed study begins with the determination of orthogonal patterns of pressure anomaly that are characteristic of geostrophic flow, computed from the averaged seasonal LATEX-A field hydrography and assumed dynamics of the system. LATEX-A shelf break mooring data then will be projected onto these patterns of variability, which we refer to as dynamic vertical structure functions or dynamic modes. Estimates of time varying pressure anomaly profiles or dynamic height are produced by the summation of weighted dynamic modes. Estimation of cross-shelf geostrophic transport follows from the pressure anomaly profiles and geostrophy.

Student Participation: None

Publications: None yet.

2.4.8 Interpretative Synthesis of Latex Shelf and Slope Circulation Patterns from Satellite and In-Situ Measurements Task 19942

Principal Investigator: Nan Walker

Status: Completed, final report issued.

MMS Relevance: The Texas-Louisiana Shelf Physical Oceanography Program (LATEX) produced valuable data sets that were beyond the scope of that project to synthesize. Among these were data pertaining to near-surface circulation. This project is a cost-effective means of maximizing the utilization of those data to gain greater insight into current dynamics. Surface and near-surface currents are of critical importance in understanding the transport of pollutants.

Project Description: The project has two parts. The first focuses on describing circulation associated with Loop eddies separated from the Loop Current during the LATEX period. The second will provide an interpretation of drifter movement relative to coastal features such as the location, movement, and longevity of shelf and slope circulation. The data sets to be explored are NOAA AVHRR sea-surface temperatures, TOPEX and ERS-1 sea-surface height data, and near-surface current measurements from the Surface Current and Lagrangian Drifter Program.

Student Participation: None

Publications: None yet.

2.4.9   An Observational and Predictive Study of Inner Shelf Currents Over the Texas-Louisiana Shelf Task 19943

Principal Investigator: William Wiseman and Normal Guinasso

Status: Ongoing.

MMS Relevance: The archived data from the Texas Automated Buoy System provides a valuable adjunct to the LATEX derived understanding of coastal currents. This study adds those data and extends TABS into Louisiana water.

Project Description: A data buoy designed to measure near-surface currents and report in near-real time, has been deployed in Louisiana waters as an extension of the Texas Automated Buoy System. Historical data from this array are to be analyzed. Development of new buoy technologies will continue during this project.

Student Participation: Y.T. Lo (Ph.D. Texas A&M) and Dr. J. She Old Dominion, Post Doct.

Publications: None yet.

2.4.10 Dynamic Height and Transport Across the Texas-Louisiana Shelf Break Task 19948

Principal Investigator: Carol Current, William J. Wiseman

Status: Completed, report issued.

Current, C.L. and W.J. Wiseman, Jr. 2000. Dynamic height and seawater transport across the Louisiana-Texas shelf break. OCS Study MMS 2000-45. U.S. Dept. of the Interior, Minerals Management Service, Gulf of Mexico OCS Region, New Orleans, LA. 46pp.

MMS Relevance: The coast of the Gulf of Mexico has many environmental and economic resources. Transport of pollutants from oil and gas activity sites has the potential of impacting other resources, especially fisheries. This project focused on the understanding and quantification of horizontal transport across the shelf break.

Project Description: The study applied dynamic modal analysis to LATEX-A mooring data to estimate time dependent, vertically resolved geostrophic transport across the Louisiana-Texas continental shelf break. The scope of the study was limited to cross-shelf geostrophic flow on the 200m isobath. Geostrophic transport profiles were found to vary smoothly with season. Offshore transport was strongest in the upper 70m of water during winter. The summer was characterized by onshore transport developing first in deeper water and progressing up the water column until prevalent from surface to the seafloor. The results contradicted previous models and suggested that an understanding of the Texas-Louisiana shelf will require understanding of the Mexican portion of the shelf.

Student Participation: None

Publication: None to date.

2.4.11 Coastal Marine Environmental Modeling Physical Oceanography I, II & III Tasks 19917, 19953 & 19965

Principal Investigator: Bill Wiseman, Masamichi Inoue, Gregory Stone, and Dubravko Justic

Status, Phase I complete report issued. Phases II and III ongoing.

Inoue, M., W. J. Wiseman, Jr. and D. Park. 1998. Coastal Marine Environmental Modeling. OCS Study MMS 98-0052. U. S. Dept. of the Interior Minerals Management Service, Gulf of Mexico OCS Region, New Orleans, La. 133 pp.

MMS Relevance: Estuaries are important coastal features, world-wide. Uses of these coastal systems present potentially conflicting demands, often requiring management based on extensive monitoring. One cost-effective alternative to extensive monitoring is modeling. Some monitoring is still required to calibrate the models, define forcing functions and boundary conditions and skill assess the model's usefulness, but the resulting savings over the cost of a complete monitoring program should be significant.

Louisiana's bar-built estuaries are broad and shallow with mean depths of only a meter or two. Tidal currents and local wind have significant impacts on these estuaries. Management decisions concerning these environments concern the dominant physical processes, sediment erosion, transport and deposition, eutrophication, and recruitment to the estuarine nursery grounds, among others. Arguably the most accurately modeled, at this time, are the physical processes. To date, though, no one has developed a modeling framework for these systems, which has been carefully calibrated, skill-assessed and applied to practical problems.

Project Description: This ongoing project has modeled hydrodynamics, sediment dynamics, and ecosystem dynamics along the Louisiana coast, a region influenced by processes occurring in both State and Federal jurisdictions. The selection of sites for modeling during this study was dependent upon the availability of existing data sets. Because of the excellent existing data sets, Terrebonne Bay, the Atchafalaya

Bay/Fourleague Bay complex, and Barataria Bay are reasonable choices for initial study. Initial results of this effort include development and calibration of a two-dimensional hydrodynamic code coupling estuarine and coastal waters. Preliminary efforts have been made to add suspended sediment dynamics, nutrient dynamics, and phytoplankton dynamics to the code. The results, when applied to a 'climatologically' forced model of Fourleague Bay, have been encouraging. Further improvements of the model parameterization are clearly necessary. It is also clear that the natural variability in external forcing (stochastic forcing) is important to realistic results from the model. Finally, our initial efforts to apply three-dimensional dynamics using the community Princeton Ocean Model have proven to be quite satisfying.

The continuing portion of the program is developing the two- and three-dimensional models, their extension to larger and more realistic shelf-estuarine coupling regions, and improvements in the ecological code, including a suspended sediment module and a marsh-flooding module. The modeling is taking a two-pronged approach. At the same time that we continue to advance our capabilities with a fully three-dimensional hydrodynamic model, we will explore the extension of the existing two-dimensional model to include a sediment dynamics module and an ecological module. Collection of field data for model formulation, calibration, and verification are, also, being undertaken.

Students: Masters, Dong Ho Park, and Mark Bi, Ph.D. Susan Welsh

Publications:

Inoue, M, and W.J. Wiseman Jr. submitted. Transport, stirring, and mixing processes in a Louisiana estuary: a model study. Geophysical Research

Inoue, M. and W. J. Wiseman, Jr. 1995. Modeling shear-flow dispersion, transport and mixing processes in Louisiana estuaries. Estuarine Research Federation 1995 Annual Meeting, Corpus Christi, TX.

Inoue, M. and W. J. Wiseman, Jr. 1995. Transport processes in Louisiana estuaries: Their importance to land loss. Geological Society of America Annual Meeting. New Orleans, LA.

Inoue, M. and W. J. Wiseman, Jr. 1996. Modeling circulation, transport, and mixing processes in Louisiana estuaries. American Geophysical Union Ocean Sciences Meeting. San Diego, CA.

Park, D., 1998. A modeling study of the Barataria Basin system. M. Sc. Thesis, Dept. Oceanography and Coastal Sciences, LSU, Baton Rouge, La. 134pp.

2.4.12 Coastal Currents of the Northern Gulf of Mexico Task 19928

Principal Investigators: William J. Wiseman, Larry J. Rouse, Jr. and S.P. Dinnel

Status: Completed final report issued.

Dinnel, S.P., Wm, J. Wiseman, Jr., and L.J. Rouse, Jr. 1996. Coastal currents in the northern Gulf of Mexico. OCS Study MMS 97-0005. U.S. Dept. of the Interior, Minerals Management Service, Gulf of Mexico OCS Region, New Orleans, La. 113 pp.

MMS Relevance: The currents responsible for the movement of contaminants (oil) on the continental shelf are predominantly along shore on the inner shelf. MMS requires statistical knowledge of these coastal currents, especially the along shore currents, in order to make strategic management and planning decisions. This project has statistically described the available surface and near-surface current meter records for the inner shelf of the northern Gulf of Mexico, described the record mean flows and the flow variability, and described along shore current maximum velocities and along shore flow persistence.

Project Description: The study area was from Dixie County, Florida, to the U.S.-Mexico international border and from the coastline seaward to a distance of 20 NM (36.5 km). Historical observations from moored current meters were statistically analyzed. Data from 12 different programs, at 47 locations were used in the analysis. All data records in 10 m. or less water depth were used. Only records in the upper half of the water column were used where water depth exceeded 10 m. Record lengths greater than 27 days were segmented into four seasons. Data were resolved into along- and cross-shore velocity components, where along shore was determined by the local coastline. Records means, variances, standard error of means, maxima and minimum, and auto-correlation time scales were computed for each seasonal record. Statistical significance levels were determined for the record means. Total record variances were compared to those of 40-hour low-passed filtered records to estimate the relative contribution of the non-tidal flow.

Flow duration and persistence statistics were calculated for each along shore record. These were the percent of flow in each direction, the number of flow events within selected speed ranges, the single event of maximum duration, and the single event of maximum estimated displacement.

Three seasons, winter, spring and fall, exhibited predominantly westward mean flows. Spring mean flows were westward on the inner shelf west of the Mississippi Delta and eastward east of the Delta. The summer season exhibited as many occurrences of westward as eastward mean flows, with a general flow reversal to the east on the south Texas inner shelf. Maximum alongshore current magnitudes exceeded maximum cross-shore current magnitudes in all seasons. Maximum alongshore currents to the west and the alongshore variance magnitude increased to the west in all seasons.

Student Involvement: none.

Publications: None as yet.

2.5 Research Area: Deepwater Environment Studies

Four projects at a cost of $810,000 were initiated in the area of deepwater environment studies. A related workshop convened by R. Carney was funded outside of the CMI structure. Two projects were literature reviews and analyses (Tasks 19904 and 19946). One involved chemical analysis of samples collected with funding from the NOAA National Undersea Research Program (Task 19946). The only program employing extensive at-sea sampling (Task 19910 as amended) is evaluating the utility of available acoustic technology for identifying geohazards and chemosynthetic habitats.

2.5.1 Development of an Ecological Overview Appropriate for Management of Resource Development in Continental Slope Habitats Task 19904

Principal Investigator: Robert S. Carney

Status: Completed Final report submitted and in revision.

MMS Relevance: MMS has an extensive history in surveying the continental shelf and conducting studies that test for OCS-related impacts. Two persistent problems with such impact studies have been (1) the lack of useful prior predictions about impact, and (2) the extreme background variation in benthic populations. As OCS activity and potential environmental impact moves into the deep-sea environment MMS is faced with vastly less understanding of that ecosystem. Since it is fiscally impossible to undertake all basic deep studies that might be of value, MMS must set priorities based upon existing information. This study carried out a broad review of basic and applied deep ecology for the purpose of identifying those areas of greater and of less MMS relevance.

Project Description: The project was both a literature review and a data reanalysis. The review was directed at a critical evaluation of ideas published in the past 20 years about deep ecology. Of special interest were those areas in which the deep system was seen as being fundamentally different than the shallow. These might represent areas where impacts could be most likely. The data reanalysis for focused on a critical comparison of the claimed results of the Northern Gulf of Mexico Continental Slope Study with results obtainable from analysis of that project's datasets.

Student involvement: Two undergraduate workers.

Publication: None yet.

2.5.2 Digital High Resolution Acoustic Data Acquisition and Processing for Improved Benthic Habitat/Geohazards Evaluations and Classification of Chemosynthetic Communities Task 19910

Principal Investigator: Harry H. Roberts

Status: Completed, final report issued.

MMS Relevance: With the increased activity on the continental slope with its inherently unstable bottom, there is greater-than-ever need to gain knowledge of the surficial geology. This study examines the potential of 3D-Seismic data to assess geohazards.

Project Description: Using high resolution acoustic data, 3D-seismic surface attribute data, and direct seafloor verification, better criteria for evaluating geohazards and protected benthic habitats will be sought. Data have been solicited from industry and acquired during the project using surface towed acoustic sources and dual channel DELPH 2 systems.

Students: Debnath Basu Ph.D

Publications: None to date.

2.5.3 Fate and Effects of Barium and Radium-Rich Fluid Emissions from Hydrocarbon Seeps on the Benthic Habitats of the Gulf of Mexico Offshore Louisiana Task 19946

Principal Investigator: Dr. Paul Aharon, D.L. Van Gent and M.L. Scott

Project Status: Completed, final report issued.

MMS Relevance: Evidence that a particular part of the ocean has been exposed to discharges from oil and gas operations has always depended upon chemical signals. Since barium is a major component in drilling mud and only a minor component of Gulf of Mexico sediments, it has been considered an excellent indicator. Dr. Ahron's work on seep systems in the Gulf has shown this to be absolutely incorrect. Seeping brines are so barium and radium rich that they produce mineral deposits on the seafloor. Clearly, barium must now be used by MMS with extreme caution. The current project examines barium and radium discharge rates.

Project Description: The work of Dr. Aharon and his colleagues on the chemistry of deepwater hydrocarbon seep environments seriously challenges two well regarded ideas about chemical contamination in the OCS due to oil and gas activity. Oil and gas development in the northern Gulf of Mexico has been widely identified as the major source of two contaminants. One is barium, which comes from drilling fluids and can be toxic. The other is radium, which is radioactive and comes from "fossil" water in petroleum deposits and is discharged into the sea. The link between oil and gas drilling and barium is thought to be so well established that barium is often used as a chemical indicator of industry contamination. It has, however, now been proven that both barium and radium are naturally emitted at certain deepwater sites associated with subsurface salt domes. This project will quantify these naturals emissions so that the contribution from oil and gas activities can be understood in a larger geochemical context.

Students: B. Fu. Ph.D.

Publications:

Fu, B. , P. Aharon, D.L. Van Gent, and L.M. Scott (1996) Anomalously high 226Ra in fluids advecting to the sea floor: A new radioactive source in the Gulf of Mexico. Gulf Coast Assoc. Geol. Soc.Trans. 46: 125-131.

Fu, B. and P. Aharon (1997) Origin and depositional model of barite deposits associated with hydrocarbon seeps on the Gulf of Mexico slope, offshore Louisiana: Gulf Coast Assoc. Geol. Soc. Trans. 47: 13-20.

Fu, B. (1998) A Study of Pore Fluids and Barite Deposits from Hydrocarbon Seeps: Deepwater Gulf of Mexico. Unpublished PhD Dissertation, Louisiana State University, 243 pp.

2.5.4 Potential Vulnerability of Fish to Deepwater Development Task 19962

Principal Investigators: Mark Benfield and Rich Shaw

Status: Ongoing.

MMS Relevance: Progression of industry beyond the continental shelf break is an established fact in the Gulf of Mexico. That progression has preceded substantial studies of the issues surround environmental impact and living resource conflicts. This study addresses that issue

Project Description: The project is a review of available information of the offshore commercial species Bluefin, yellow fin, black fin tuna, wahoo, blue marlin, two species of flying fish, ocean sunfish, dolphin fish, blue runners, and the sargassum community.

Student Participation: Beth Burroughs (MS)

Publications: None yet.

2.6   Research Areas: Socioeconomics & Policy

A total of 16 research projects and one workshop at a MMS cost of $2,225,000. And equal LSU match has been initiated in the area of socioeconomics dealing with OCS impacts upon the human community. The CMI projects represent a major proportion of the total Gulf of Mexico region effort in this area. CMI and its URI predecessor were fortuitous in their timing. They began during a marked depression in OCS activities and were in place during the boom associated with deep-water development. Accordingly, two themes have been recurrent, (1) the socioeconomic impact of industry restructuring during the bust until 1996, and (2) the boom impacts of increased deep-water activity after that date.

While the first two projects in this area (Tasks 19902 and 19903) continued the URI pattern of supporting interview and assessment of conventional wisdom, subsequent projects have been more quantitative. Seven have been primarily economic (Tasks 19906, 19913, 19923, 19934, 19945, 19955, and 19967). Most of the investigators in these economic projects have been in the Center for Energy Studies at LSU. An equal number of projects have been largely sociological (Tasks 19929, 19939, 19941, 19951, 19954, 19957, and 19966), depending more heavily on demographic analysis than interview. Most of the investigators in these sociology projects have been in the Department of Sociology at LSU.

An extremely important aspect of the Socioeconomic projects undertaken as part of the CMI project has been the development of the Louisiana Population Data Center. Housed in the Sociology Department at LSU, the Center was initiated in 1987. The existence of the Center has made it possible for MMS to effectively meet its sociological information needs in Louisiana. At the same time, the substantial support from MMS for the Center has greatly increased its effectiveness. State support for this Center has been important in meeting the CMI matching obligation.

2.6.1   Socioeconomic Outer Continental Shelf Issue Analysis of Stakeholders in the Central Gulf of Mexico Task 19902

Principal Investigator: Robert Grambling

Status: Completed, final report issued.

MMS Relevance: This report summarized the research effort and findings of an investigation of the issues associated with Outer Continental Shelf (OCS) oil and gas activities in the Central Gulf of Mexico. Stakeholders assessed for the delineation of the issues associated with OCS oil and gas activities ranged across the offshore oil and gas industry; the offshore support sector; other direct and indirect coastal users; stakeholders that benefited from economic growth in general; concerned citizen groups, and public and Government organizations.

Project Description: Through the study 131 individuals in coastal communities of Alabama, Mississippi and Louisiana were interviewed concerning their perspectives on offshore oil and gas development. Census data at the county and community level were also examined, but in the end combined knowledge of coastal communities in Louisiana, Mississippi, and Alabama proved more useful. Snowball sampling was used it is a method through which the researcher develops an ever-increasing set of sample observations. One respondent in the sample under study is asked to recommend others for interviewing, and each of the subsequently interviewed participants is asked for further recommendations.

Positive and negative issues emerged across the States surveyed. While jobs and economic spin-offs emerged as issues in all regions they were more frequently mentioned in Louisiana. Negative economic impacts also came out as issues across the three States, but were more closely associated with the coastal tourism region of Alabama. There were marked differences in the issues associated with regulating OCS activities with Louisiana respondents maintaining that the activity was too heavily regulated and Mississippi and Alabama respondents maintaining that careful regulation was necessary. There were also marked differences in the extent to which aesthetic considerations emerged as issues. In Louisiana aesthetic consideration did not emerge as an issue, while in Mississippi and Alabama they did.

Student Participation: Not reported.

Publications: Not reported.

2.6.2 Characteristics and Possible Impacts of a Restructured OCS Oil and Gas Industry in the Gulf of Mexico Task 19903

Principal Investigator: Shirley Laska

Status: Completed, final report issued.

Seydlitz,R. and S. Laska. 1995. Characteristics and Possible Impacts of a Restructured OCS Oil and Gas Industry in the Gulf of Mexico. OCS Study MMS 95-0055. Minerals Management Service, U.S. Dept. of Interior. Gulf of Mexico OCS Region. New Orleans, La.

MMS Relevance: The restructuring of the OCS industry, a shift from major corporations to minors, is a pervasive trend in the Gulf of Mexico with many possible implications. This study examines the sociological impacts.

Project Description: There were two data collection phases. Their first was an exploratory study of 11 significant major corporations and independent companies employing face-to-face interviews with key representatives. The results were used to construct an interview instrument, which was used in the second phase. The second phase was telephone interviews with executives from five types of offshore companies.

The companies were selected by random sampling. The interviews consisted of open-ended questions concerning the companies' characteristics and use of service firms in the fall of 1994 and in 1986; the executives' predictions about the future of the oil and gas industry in the offshore Gulf; and the influences of leasing policies, technological developments, Federal agencies, and environmental regulations on the companies' practices in the Gulf.

The results revealed that there are five distinct types of companies operating in the Gulf: major cooperation, large and small integrated independent firms, and large and small nonintegrated independent companies. The findings also suggested that six trends are occurring. First, there was an increase in the number of companies operating in the Gulf between 1986 and the fall of 1994. Second, most of the companies obtained more oil and gas in 1993 than in 1986. Third, most of the firms were more involved in exploration in the Gulf in 1994 than in 1986. Fourth, participation in joint ventures increased between 1986 and the fall of 1994. Fifth, changes in the companies' activities suggested a tendency toward becoming involved in downstream integration operations. Sixth, changes in characteristics, views of the business environment and practices implied that a shift is occurring in activity in the Gulf: the nonintegrated independent businesses are becoming more involved while the major and integrated independent companies are maintaining a steady rate of activity or reducing their involvement.

Student Participation: Not reported.

Publications: Not reported.

2.6.3 Modeling the Behavior of Integrated Companies: Implications for Offshore Gas Development and Policies Task 19906

Principal Investigator: Alan Pulsipher

Status: Completed, final report issued.

MMS Relevance: Minerals Management Service (MMS) has expressed concern about how a shift from the majors to independents will affect the pace of exploration drilling as opposed to development drilling, and whether independents are financially stable enough to support offshore drilling. In the past decade the "majors" (integrated oil and gas producing, refining and marketing companies) have been shifting their exploration and production focus to foreign countries. Between 1981 and 1991 the share of production from the Gulf of Mexico OCS attributable to independent producers (that do not refine or market) has increased from 17.5 percent to 28 percent and in 1991 independents installed over 70 percent of the new drilling platforms in the Gulf of Mexico. The conventional wisdom about the magnitude and permanence as well as the causes and effects of this transition is still evolving. Is it truly a transition, or an illusion created by the integrated companies reacting more rapidly to an overall decline in the profitability of domestic oil and gas production? Are the independents "taking over" or does it just appear so because their share increases as the majors leave?

The trends in E&D expenditures, which have been frequently used to describe the apparent "take over" of domestic oil and gas activities by the independents, seem clear and dramatic. Over the period 1987 to 1992, the domestic E&D expenditures by the majors declined 34 percent while those by the independents increased by about 12 percent. However, data on E&D spending on foreign prospects indicate that both the majors and the independents have responded aggressively to opportunities abroad. Foreign E&D expenditures by the majors increased by an impressive 113 percent, while expenditures abroad by the independents also increased by a healthy 73 percent. The differences in expenditure effectiveness between the two groups of firms seem to narrow with time and the averages have become too close over the last three years to support any generalizations about differences in effectiveness regarding domestic and foreign activity.

The simple descriptive statistics of upstream oil and gas industry indicators developed indicate that independents have been both more aggressive and more successful than the majors in exploration, while the majors have only been moderately more successful than independents in development drilling on the OCS. In the aggregate, both the large and smaller independents have been at least marginally more effective than the majors in adding hydrocarbon reserves per successful foot drilled. On average for every foot of successful well drilled by the majors on the OCS, 227 barrels of oil equivalent (BOE) of new hydrocarbon reserves were added to original recoverable hydrocarbons in place during the period 1983-1992. Whereas the independents added 265 BOE (large independents added 242 BOE while smaller independents added 312 BOE) of hydrocarbons for every foot of successful wells drilled during the same period. However, if drilling effectiveness were calculated using total footage drilled in the denominator rather than successful footage drilled the difference narrows. Majors added 106 BOE per foot drilled while independents as a group added 111 BOE. But within the independent classification, large independents added 104 BOE per foot and smaller independents 125 BOE per foot drilled.

It was found that the large independent firms on average have a negatively elastic drilling response of -1.62 to changes in the average effective tax rate compared to negative inelastic drilling response of -0.86 by the majors to taxes. The smaller independents have a negative elastic drilling response of -1.33 to taxes. A point estimate of drilling elasticity with respect to economic incentives among firms of different sizes was found to be statistically identical (0.42) in the Gulf OCS region. The effectiveness of the majors in adding new reserves per drilling effort seems to be more negatively affected by resource depletion than is the case for either the large or smaller independents. The response of drilling effectiveness to depletion among the majors is significantly elastic, whereas the effectiveness among the large and smaller independents is significantly inelastic in the region

Publications:

Pulsipher, Allan G.; Iledare, O. O.; and Baumann, R. H. 1994. Modeling the structure and performance of integrated and independent producers; implications for offshore oil and gas development. Annual Report Submitted to Minerals Management Service, New Orleans, LA. November 16.

Iledare, O. O.; Pulsipher A. G.; and Baumann, R. H. (1994). Firm Size and the development of petroleum resources on the U.S. Gulf of Mexico. Proceeding, 16th USAEE/IAEE Annual North American Conference, Dallas, TX, November 6-9.

Iledare, O. O.; Pulsipher, A. G.; and Baumann, R. H. (1995). Effects of an increasing role for independents on petroleum resource development on the Gulf of Mexico OCS. The Energy Journal 16(2), pp. 59-76.

2.6.4 A Socioeconomic Baseline Study for the Gulf of Mexico, Phase I Task 19913

Principal Investigator: Joachim Singleman, Forrest A. Deseran, and Charles M. Tolbert

Status: Completed, no separate final report issued.

MMS Relevance: Oil and gas production in rural areas has the potential of setting up boom-bust counter cycles. Concerns about such impacts, however, are poorly supported by rigorously collected demographic data. This trial project uses coastal Louisiana as a proving ground for development of appropriate demographic data extracted from U.S. Census files. This trial effort may be extended Gulf Wide.

Project Description: The project developed a regional database extracted from the U.S. Census. Analysis focused upon three objectives: (1) estimating performance indices, (2) testing the robustness of performance models across the boom-bust cycles, and (3) modeling the overall effect of oil prices and drilling activity on Louisiana parishes.

Student Involvement: Post Doctoral Natsumi Aratame, Graduate Kuo-Hua Chen

Publications: None yet.

2.6.5 The Environmental and Safety Risks of Increasing Activity by Independents on the Federal Outer Continental Shelf Task 19923

Principal Investigator: Alan Pulsipher

Status: Completed, final report issued.

MMS Relevance: Smaller independent oil producers are now doing more of the exploration and production (E&P) of offshore oil and gas reserves in the Gulf of Mexico due to the apparent refocusing of E&P activities and investments abroad by majors and larger independents in the early 1990s. As a result, both industry and regulatory analysts have expressed concern that this trend will increase the risk of more accidents and oil spills in the Gulf. The premise underlying such apprehension was that smaller independent companies do not have the majors' technical, scientific, or regulatory skills. Therefore the objective of this study was to ascertain if there is an empirical justification for such apprehension. As the study progressed it also seemed appropriate and efficient to use our data to determine if the Minerals Management Service's (MMS) safety and platform inspection programs have reduced the frequency or severity of accidents or spills in the Gulf. The questions asked were: Is there persuasive evidence that an expanded role for smaller independents on the OCS would: 1) hinder the pace or effectiveness of petroleum resource development, and 2) pose greater environmental and safety risks?

Project Summary: For analytical purposes, oil and gas operators operating in the U.S have been classified into three groups. Majors are integrated companies with more than 1 billion BOE in petroleum reserves worldwide. Large independents are those firms cited in the Oil and Gas Journal (OGJ) list of the largest 100 firms that are not majors, but have assets of at least $500 million. Smaller independent firms are those appearing on the OGJ list of the largest 300 firms but do not have assets of $500 million or more.

The primary sources of information used in this study were the MMS events and platform inspection files. The events file contains narrative and numerical information on unplanned or unexpected incidents relating to: 1) environmental damage or upset; 2) workplace accidents resulting in bodily injury, illness, disease, or death. Accident data include cause, e.g., loss of well control, spills, fires, explosions, loss of structure, and collision. Comparable data on violations of operating orders (recorded as instances of noncompliance of "INCs") are available from MMS' platform inspection data system. These data were organized on an operator-by-operator basis.

Descriptive statistics were used to compare environmental and safety records by reviewing the types and causes of safety and environmental events and analyzing measurable effects of each event in terms of deaths and injuries sustained, lost time, pollution spills, and property damage. Measurable indicators of operator performance were defined, such as nominal, weighted and relative accident and spill rates. These rates were used to measure trends in safety and environmental performance of majors and independents in OCS E&P operations.

Associations among accidents, spills, and several hypothesized explanatory variables (average platform age, type of operation, effectiveness of regulation and its enforcement, and firm size) were examine by regression. The effects of these factors on accidents and spills in oil and gas E&P operations were evaluated using a panel data set of firms classified as majors, large and small independents over the period 1987 - 1993. Using this data, we estimated a Tobit specification of accidents and spill rates. The study also attempted to use weighted least squares regression analysis to evaluate the impact of "bad actors" (firms with significantly worse than average accident and spill records) on the industry-wide statistics.

The analysis is relevant to MMS policy and program planning only insofar as proposals for new policies or changes in policies are driven by the premise that a larger role for smaller, independent firms poses new or heightened risks to worker safety or the environment. Statistical and descriptive analyses of recorded accidents and oil spills in the MMS event file provide little evidence to support this premise. In fact, simple comparisons indicate that independents have performed better than the majors, and if this performance were to be maintained, the independents should not pose additional risks to workers or the environment. Further, it is evident from our econometric results that the aging of operating platforms, firm-specific effects, year-specific effects and safety and inspection programs of the Minerals Management Services (MMS) significantly, in a statistical sense, affect accidents or oil spills during E&P operation. This finding may be relevant for MMS's ongoing efforts to develop standards for "re-qualifying"older platforms.

Student Participation: Graduate Students, Dmitry Mesyanzhinov (Ph.D)

Publications:

Pulsipher A. G., Iledare, O. O., Baumann, R.H., and D. Mesyanzhinov. 1995. Operating
        Performance and Environmental and Safety Risks: A Preliminary Comparison

of Majors and Independents. Offshore and Arctic Operations 1995, PD-Vol. 68, pp. 219-228.

Pulsipher A. G., Iledare, O. O., Dismukes, D. E., Mesyanzhinov, D. and R. H. Baumann. 1996. Comparing the Safety and Environmental Records of Firms Operating Offshore Platforms in the Gulf of Mexico. Proceedings of the Energy Week `96 Conference, Book III pp. 405-408.

Iledare, O. O., Pulsipher A. G., Dismukes, D. E., and R. H. Baumann. 1996. Safety Regulations, Firm Size, and the Risk of Accidents in E&P Operations on the Gulf of Mexico Outer Continental Shelf (OCS)." SPE Paper # 35934 Presented at the Society of Petroleum Engineers third International Conference on Health, Safety, and Environment in Oil and Gas Exploration and Production held in New Orleans, June 9 - 12, 1996

Iledare, Omowumi O., Pulsipher Allan G., Dismukes, David E. and Dmitry Mesyanzhinov. 1997. "Oil spills, workplace safety and firm size: evidence from the U.S. Gulf of Mexico OCS." The Energy Journal, 18 (4):73-89

2.6.6 Oil and Gas Development & Coastal Income Inequality Task 19929

Principal Investigator: Charles Tolbert and Edward Shihadeh

Status: Final report incorporated with Task 19941.

MMS Relevance: A place-level comparative analysis of family income inequality is proposed that builds on recently completed work at the parish level. The parish-level research has generated useful results and considerable interest among representatives of various Federal and State agencies. Yet, the research is obviously limited by the size and diversity of parishes that can mask important variation within parishes. The proposed research would improve on the current inequality analysis by employing data on places (urbanized areas of 2500 or more persons) from the 1970, 1980, and 1990 Censuses.

Project Description: The focus of the analysis will be trends in family income inequality in coastal Louisiana places near and adjacent to the substantially developed Outer Continental Shelf (OCS). Like the recently concluded parish-level project, the proposed comparative analysis design permits inequality trends in Louisiana places to be compared to inequality trends in coastal places of the Florida panhandle where there has been no significant OCS development. Quantitative techniques will be used to match Louisiana and Florida places as precisely as possible on important baseline (1970) demographic, industrial, and occupational factors.

Inequality trends along the Gulf of Mexico will also be compared to Statewide family income inequality in Louisiana and Florida and to national inequality levels. The proposed analysis design also permits a temporal comparison across key decades in the recent history of the offshore oil and gas industries. While the decade of the 1970s was one of rising oil prices and greatly expanded OCS development, the 1980s saw prices fall and offshore activity generally decline. This change in development patterns is an important reason to study inequality trends in the 1970-1980 and 1980-1990 periods. Following conventions of inequality analysis, trends in family income inequality will be gauged with multiple measures of inequality computed with decennial census data. The inequality will then be modeled to control for exogenous factors that could be sources of variation in local inequality patterns. In these ways, the analysis is designed to gain an understanding of the effects of OCS development on income inequality in coastal areas.

Student Participation: Undergraduate 1, graduate Rebecca Carter and Graham Ousey

Publications: None yet.

2.6.7 Forecasting of the Number of Platform Installed, Removed and Operated on the Gulf of Mexico OCS Task 19934

Principal Investigators: Allan G. Pulsipher, Omowumi O. Iledare, and Robert Bauman

Status: Completed, final report issued.

MMS Relevance: A systematic examination of numbers, costs and disposal options of aging offshore structures has not been conducted since 1984. That study by the National Research Council Marine board relied heavily on opinion and extrapolation. The current study provides MMS with an updated and fact-based assessment. The models to be developed in this study will allow objective review of policy and revision if necessary.

Project Description: A model was being developed which allows better forecasting of the inventory of oil and gas structures in the Gulf of Mexico for the next 25 years.

Student Participation: Ph.D Qiaozhen Lucy Zhu

2.6.8 Commuting, Migration, and Offshore Oil/Gas Extraction Task 19939

Principal Investigators: Joachim Singleman, and Natsumi Aratame

Status, Ongoing

MMS Relevance: Prior MMS research has documented the impact (benefit and cost) of OCS activities on coastal populations. The link to inland populations, however, remains unexplored.

Project Description: The project analyzes the commuting and migration patterns in relationship to OCS activities. Offshore employment often requires a one-three week work pattern making it feasible for workers to commute over unusually long distances. As a result, measurement of labor migration alone into the OCS region can not capture the entire workforce impact. Effective models of the socioeconomic impact of OCS activities must, therefore, include both commuting and migration.

Five major sources of data are being utilized:

    1. The 1960-90 Census commute-to-work files.

    2. The 1990 Journey-to-work data for metropolitan areas.

    3. The 1985-90 Census county-to-county migration file.

    4. The 1990 Public Use Microdata Sample.

    5. The Socioeconomic Database for the coastal States maintained at LSU.

Methods include graphical representation, commuting/migration patterns, statistical analyses, and analysis of social and welfare indices.

Graduate Student, 1 unnamed.

Publications: None yet.

2.6.9 Sustainable Socioeconomic Development in Oil and Gas Country: A Case Study of Abbeville, Louisiana Task 19941

Principal Investigators: Charles M. Tolbert, Edward S. Shihadeh, and Deborah Tootle.

Status: Completed, report pending review.

MMS Relevance: Offshore oil and gas development impacts coastal populations in many ways, producing costs and well as benefits. When development follows boom-bust cycles, costs and benefits may become out of phase resulting in extended periods where costs exceed benefits. Abbeville, Louisiana is a small coastal community partially dependent upon offshore development. It has experienced the industry's boom-bust cycles without major deleterious impact. If MMS develops an understanding of those factors that allow this local economy to remain robust, it may be able to minimize boom-bust impacts elsewhere.

Project Description: Non-metropolitan areas are typically dominated by a single industrial sector, leaving them vulnerable to business cycles. Abbeville, Louisiana is such a non-metropolitan area, but one that appears to have been minimally effected by oil and gas industry variation. This may be due to a combination of economic diversification and social characteristics. The project is an in-depth, multi-level, multi-method case study of Abbeville that asks four questions.

1. How diversified is the local economy?

2. Are there social relationships and processes that cushion the effects of economic downturn?

3. What was the role of local leadership is structuring the robust economy.

4. Does the neighborhood dispersion of socioeconomic and industrial characteristics contribute to the stability of the economy?

Methods include guided conversations of stakeholders and community leaders. Supplemental data will be obtained from the Abbeville-Vermilion Parish Chamber of Commerce, and the Meridional (newspaper dating to 1850).

Graduate Students: 2

Publications: None yet.

2.6.10 Impacts of Infrastructure of Port Fourchon Associated with Deep Oil and Gas Developments Task 19945

Principal Investigator: Walter Keithley and Don Hughes

Status: Part 1 completed, Part 2 pending.

MMS Relevance: Deep-water oil and gas development has caused a marked increase of heavy truck traffic to Pt. Fourchon, Louisiana. The transportation infrastructure along Louisiana highway 1 from US 90 to Pt. Fourchon was never intended for this load. As an unexpected economic impact to the region from OCS activity, MMS needs to quantify the cost.

Project Description: LSU in cooperation with the Fourchon Port Authority has initiated a traffic count an analysis along Louisiana Highway 1. That count will be incorporated into economic models to develop an estimate of costs.

Student Participation: 1 undergraduate

Publications: None yet.

2.6.11 Labor Demand in the Offshore Oil and Gas Industry/ Employment in the Offshore Oil and Gas Industry: The Louisiana Case Task 19951

Principal Investigator: Forrest A. Deseran and Debora Tootle

Status: Ongoing.

MMS Relevance: In 1997 the oil and gas industry in coastal Louisiana had experienced a resurgence, local employment impact appeared to be minimal, yet there was a worker shortage. Such a response is counter to expectations developed from boom-bust models for the industry. MMS needs to understand this departure from expectations.

Project Description: The project examines three questions about the factors associated with low local employment rates in the oil and gas industry.

1. What causes qualified worker shortage?

2. What are the consequences to regional economies and the industry due to low employment?

3. What local strategies can be adopted to address the imbalance of labor supply and demand?

Student Participation: Ph.D. Linda Tobin and Terry Estes

Publications: None yet.

2.6.12 Job Loss and Reemployment of Women and Blacks in Louisiana Coastal Communities Task 19954

Principal Investigator: Jochiam Singleman

Status: Ongoing

MMS Relevance: Studying job loss and reemployment not only tells MMS about labor market response to cyclical downturns, but it will also helps to understand the extent to which vulnerable groups of workers, such as young black males, are more susceptible to long-term job loss as the national and local economy undergoes industrial and spatial restructuring, using OCS activities as an example. Delineating the effect of industrial and occupational specialization of the labor market vs. human capital endowment will provide useful information to private and public institutions in planning strategies to cope with the long-term effects of structural changes hidden in cyclical patterns of expansion and contraction

Project Description: This project investigates changes in the employment status of black and women in coastal communities in Louisiana and other Gulf of Mexico States. First, we will estimate aggregate effects of changes in the industrial and occupational structure of the region. To this end, we will use shift-share analysis to examine the effects of gender segregation by industry and occupation on 1980-1990 growth in male and female employment. However, since labor market segmentation theories suggest that race and gender segregation by industry and occupation is associated with human capital differentials, we will also explore race and gender differences in the probability of experiencing job loss and reemployment after job displacement. Such changes in employment status underpin differences in employment growth for men, women, blacks and whites. Groups with a higher probability of losing a job and a lower probability of finding reemployment are more likely to have a lower rate of employment growth, all else equal. To estimate race-specific and gender-specific probabilities of job loss and reemployment, we will use multivariate regression techniques and associated methods for decomposition of the effect of individual characteristics vs. structural factors.

Student Participation: One graduate student.

2.6.13 Economic and Social Consequences of the Oil Spill at Lake Barre Task 19955

Principal Investigator: Alan Pulsipher

Status: Completed, final report issued

MMS Relevance: The Project should provide 1) a point of comparison and guide for evaluating future clean up efforts and their associated economic and social consequence, and 2) a template for studying the economic and social effects of oil spills in coastal regions and communities.

Project Description: The 5,000 barrel oil spill in Lake Barre on May 13, 1997, resulting from the rupture of a Texaco pipeline, provides an interesting opportunity to study the economic and social consequences of a major oil spill in a major Gulf Coast petroleum producing area. The Center for Energy Studies at Louisiana State University in cooperation with the Department of Sociology proposes to study these aspects of the spill directly and expeditiously, while the experience and any lessons to be learned from it are fresh in the minds of those who were involved or affected.

A great deal has been written about oil spills. But the vast preponderance has been devoted to techniques for containing and mitigating spills or their ecological and environmental effects. A literature search of the joint EPA, API, and Coast Guard sponsored Biannual Oil Spill Conferences did not find a single paper devoted to: 1) the internal response by the company responsible for the spill, 2) the direct, short-term economic and social effects on the surrounding economy, labor market, and public service infrastructure, or 3) the longer-term effects on local industries such as fishing, shrimping or oystering.

The objective of the proposed research is to begin to fill the 'economic and social effects gap' in the oil spill literature with a detailed and objective case study of the economic and social effects, both positive and negative, of the May 18, 1997, Lake Barre oil spill. This spill is a promising case study because it was large enough to test the internal oil-spill-response structure of the responsible company, Texaco, and the relevant State and local agencies and Governments but not so large as to be a catastrophic event lying outside the bounds of planning or expected contingencies. Further, the clean-up effort was praised by some as speedy and efficient.

Special attention will be paid to positive as well as negative effects. Background or baseline economic and social data will be compiled from existing databases. Discussions with business and community leaders in the area affected by the clean up will be used to collect information concerning the effects of the spills on communities and individuals in the area. Information on the mix of skills used during the clean up, and how they were mobilized to deal with this spill, will be collected from Texaco and its cooperating contractors.

Student Participation: None

2.6.14 An Analysis of the Socioeconomic Effects of OCS Activities on Ports and Surrounding Areas in the Gulf of Mexico Region Task 19957

Principal Investigator: Jochiam Singleman

Status: Ongoing.

MMS Relevance: Ports represent a special socioeconomic situation with respect to rural communities impacted by OCS activities due to the very large infrastructure costs. This is especially the case with transportation associated infrastructure. As ports like Pt. Fourchon grow, while others like Houma decline, there may be considerable socioeconomic impact and calls for the Federal Government to bear infrastructure costs. This study will examine those impacts.

Project Description: This project investigates changes in the employment status of black and women in coastal communities in Louisiana and other Gulf of Mexico States. First, we will estimate aggregate effects of changes in the industrial and occupational structure of the region. To this end, we will use shift-share analysis to examine the effects of gender segregation by industry and occupation on 1980-1990 growth in male and female employment. However, since labor market segmentation theories suggest that race and gender segregation by industry and occupation is associated with human capital differentials, we will also explore race and gender differences in the probability of experiencing job loss and reemployment after job displacement. Such changes in employment status underpin differences in employment growth for men, women, blacks and whites. Groups with a higher probability of losing a job and a lower probability of finding reemployment are more likely to have a lower rate of employment growth, all else equal. To estimate race-specific and gender-specific probabilities of job loss and reemployment, we will use multivariate regression techniques and associated methods for decomposition of the effect of individual characteristics vs. structural factors.

Student Participation: None yet.

Publications: None yet.

2.6.15 Coastal Division of Industrial Labor Over Time and Space: Continuation and Expansion of a Community Study Task 19966

Principal Investigators: Charles Tolbert, Deborha Tootle, Edward S. Shihadeh, and John J. Beggs

Status: Ongoing.

MMS Relevance: During task 19951 it was found that Abbeville, Louisiana had an economy that was robust during OCS boom-bust cycles due to industrial diversification. However, that diversification is threatened by anticipated closure of a clothing plant. If MMS is to understand these resilient local economies in the coastal region, then longitudinal studies must be undertaken of the Abbeville case, and a wider geographic coverage obtained by means of census data analysis.

Project Description: Community field study techniques are being focused upon Abbeville Louisiana and well as confidential longitudinal establishment data. These will determine the distribution of coastal industrial labor over time and space. To increase the geographic basis of the study, microdata of the US Bureau of the Census are being examined.

Student Participation: None at this time.

Publications: None at this time.

2.6.16 Economic Impact Analysis of OCS Activity Task 19967

Principal Investigators: David Dismukes, Dmitry V. Mesyazhinov, and David Hughes

Status: Ongoing.

MMS Relevance: Small changes in MMS policy or Industry development in the OCS can have major economic impact in coastal regions. Making decisions that minimize negative impacts requires an objective base for prediction and analysis. The model developed in this project provides such a tool to MMS.

Description: Development of an economic impact model that examines and quantifies the impact that increased oil and gas production activities on coastal regions.

Student Involvement: Post Doc Dr. William Olatubi, Ph.D., Mr. James Ngugana

2.7 CMI Management

Management of the initial six years of CMI has been under the direction of Dr. Robert Carney with the assistance of Madolyn Cox, and one student worker. Management has been supported under Task 19918.

APPENDIX of CMI Researchers

1.1   Aharon, Paul

Dr Aharon is a professor in the department of Geology and Geophysics at The University of Alabama, having left LSU in 2000. He came to LSU in 1982 after receiving his PhD at Hebrew University of Jerusalem and pursuing postdoctoral studies as a Queen's Fellow in Marine Sciences at the Australian National University. He established the LSU stable isotope facility in Geology and Geophysics. The CMI program represents Dr. Aharon's introduction to applied studies of oil and gas activity in the OCS.

Selected Publications:

Aharon, P. 1994. Geology and biology of modern and ancient submarine hydrocarbon seeps and vents: An Introduction. Geo-Marine Letters 14, 69-73
Aharon, P. 1994. Carbon and oxygen isotope tracers of submarine hydrocarbon emissions: Northern Gulf of Mexico. Isr. J. Earth Sci. 43, 157-164
Fu, B., Aharon, P., Van Gent, D.L., and Scott, L.M. 1996. Anomalously high 226Ra in fluids advecting to the sea floor: A new radioactive source in the Gulf of Mexico. GCAGS Trans. 46: 125-131
Aharon, P., Schwarcz, H.P. and Roberts, H.H. 1997. Radiometric dating of submarine hydrocarbon seeps in the Gulf of Mexico. Geol. Soc. Am.Bull. 109 (5): 568-579.
Wheeler, C.W. and Aharon, P. 1997. The geology and hydrogeology of Niue, South Pacific. In: (Vacher, L. and Quinn, T. eds.) Geology and Hydrogeology of Carbonate Islands, Developments in Sedimentology 54, Elsevier Science, Amsterdam, Ch. 31: 540-562

1.2   Aratame, Natsumi

Dr. Natsumi is a postdoctoral student in the Dept. of Sociology at LSU. He received his Ph.D. in sociology at the University of Chicago. His research interests include urban sociology, demography as applied to urbanization and migration, race, labor markets, social mobility, and analytical methods.

Selected Publications:

Natsumi, A., 1989. Slums in the Philippines: a case study of thr slums with potential unrest. In. K. Niitsu (ed.) Slums in contemporary Asia: The study of cities in developing countries. Akashi Syoten, Tokyo (in Japanese).
Natsumi, A. and K. Hara. 1984. Slums in Manila: slum dwellers with high asperiations. Ajia Keizai 25:113-131.

1.3   Bauman Robert

Robert H. Baumann is a senior fellow and past director at the LSU Center for Energy Studies. He also serves as Managing Director of the Central Gulf Region, Petroleum Technology Transfer Council. Baumann currently serves by appointment of the Governor as Louisiana's representative to the Natural Resources Committee of the Interstate Oil and Gas Compact Commission and is technical advisor to Governor Mike Foster's Energy

Commission; he also served in that capacity to Governors Edwards and Roemer. He received his B.A (biology) from the University of Rhode Island and his M.S. from Louisiana State University (physical geography/geomorphology with a minor in marine sciences). He is the author of more than 40 articles on energy and environmental topics.

1.4   Beggs, John J.

Dr. Beggs, Assoc Professor in LSU department of Sociology and a researcher at the Louisiana Population Data Center. He received his Ph.D. from the State Univ Ill at Chicago. His area of interest is labor issues in sociology.

Selected Publications:

Wesley Shrum and John J. Beggs. 1997. "Measuring the Network Structure of Scientific
        Organizations." Knowledge and Society 9(4).
John J. Beggs, Wayne J. Villemez, and Ruth Arnold. 1997. "Black Population Concentration
        and Black-White Inequality: Expanding the Consideration of Place and Space
        Effects." Social Forces 76:65-92.
John J. Beggs and Jeanne S. Hurlbert. 1997. "The Social Context of Job Search Ties:
        Voluntary Organization Memberships, Social Resources, and Search Outcomes."
        Sociological Perspectives 40:601-622.
John J. Beggs, Valerie A. Haines, and Jeanne S. Hurlbert. 1996. "Community Attachment in a
        Rural Setting: A Refinement and Empirical Test of the Systemic Model." Rural
        Sociology 61.

1.5   Benfield, Mark C.
Dr. Benfield is an assistant professor in the Dept. of Oceanography and Coastal Sciences at LSU. He began CMI work while a postdoctoral fellow in the Coastal Fisheries Institute. He received his B.S. at the University of Toronto and an M.S. at the University of Natal. He received his Ph.D. from Texas A&M, but did postdoctoral work at Woods Hole Oceanographic. His research interests include zooplankton ecology and image-based data systems.

Selected Publications:

Benfield, M.C., C.S. Davis and S.M. Gallager.2000. Estimating the in-situ orientation of
        Calanus finmarchicus on Georges Bank using the Video Plankton Recorder. Plankton
        Biology and Ecology, 47: 30-33.
Carvalho, R.C., M.C. Benfield and P.H. Santschi. 1999. Comparative bioaccumulation studies
        of colloidally-complexed and free-ionic metals in juvenile brown shrimp Penaeus
        aztecus (Crustacea:Decapoda:Penaeidae). Limnol. Oceanogr., 44:403-414.
Benfield, M.C., P.H. Wiebe, T.K. Stanton, C.S. Davis, S.M. Gallager and C.H.Greene. 1998.
        Estimating the spatial distribution of zooplankton biomass by combining Video
        Plankton Recorder and single-frequency acoustic data. Deep-Sea Research Part II, 45:
        1175-1199.

1.6   Braud, DeWitt

Mr Braud is a Instructor and Manager III in the Department of Geography and Anthropology at LSU. He received a BS in geography from LSU in 1971 and a MA in geography from Michigan State in 1971. He has worked broadly in the area of remote sensing and GIS, becoming associated with LSU's efforts in those areas in the early 1980's

1.7   Carman, Kevin

Dr. Carman is an associate Professor in the LSU Dept. of Biological Sciences. He received his Ph.D. from Florida State University. His area of expertise is meiofauna and microbial foodwebs

Selected Publications:

Carman, K.R., Fleeger, J.W., and S.M. Pomarico. In press. Response of a benthic food web to hydrocarbon contamination. Limnology and Oceanography

Carman, K.R. and F.C. Dobbs. 1997. Epibiotic microorganisms on copepods and other aquatic crustaceans. Microscopy Research and Technique 37: 116-135.

Pace, M.C. and K.R. Carman. 1996. Interspecific differences among meiobenthic copepods in the use of microalgal food resources. Marine Ecology Progress Series. 143: 77-86.

Carman, K.R., Fleeger, J.W., Means, J.C., Pomarico, S.M., and McMillin, D.J. 1995. Experimental investigation of the effects of polynuclear aromatic hydrocarbons on an estuarine sediment food web. Marine Environmental Research 40: 289-318.

1.8   Carney, Robert

Dr. Carney was the founding director of the CMI program at LSU, having previously served as chairman of the University Research Initiative. He is an associate professor in the LSU Dept. of Oceanography and Coastal Science and past director of the Coastal Studies Institute. He received his Ph.D. from Oregon State, M.S. from Texas A&M, and B.S. from Duke. His interests include deep-sea benthic ecology and rigorous design and analysis of environmental survey data.

Selected Publications:

MacAvoy, S, R. Carney, S. MacAvoy, and C. Fisher. In Press. Assessment of trophic links between Hydrocarbon Seep Chemosynthetic Productivity and Trapped Predator/Scavengers.. Marine Ecology Progress Series.

Rabalais, N. N., R. S. Carney and E. G. Escobar-Briones 1999. Overview of continental shelf benthic communities of the Gulf of Mexico. Sherman, K. (ed.), The Gulf of Mexico, A Large Marine Ecosystem, Blackwell Science.

Roberts H.H. and R.S. Carney. 1997. Evidence of episodic fluid, gas, and sediment venting on the northern Gulf of Mexico Continental Slope. Economic Geology 9:863-879.

1.9   Catallo, James

Dr. Catallo is an associate professor in the LSU school of Veternary Science. He received his Ph.D. from the University of William and Mary, his MS. From LSU and his B.S. from Tulane University. His research interests include: Chromatography; organic mass spectrometry; electrochemistry; molecular modeling of organic chemicals, ecotoxicology; time series/spectral analysis of ecological process signals; sediment microbiology/chemistry; ecosystem restoration/remediation; geochronology; polycyclic aromatic hydrocarbon and N-,O-, S- heterocyclic chemistry.

Selected Publications:

Catallo, W. J. 1999. Hourly and daily variation of sediment redox potential in tidal wetland sediments. USGS Biological Resources Division, Biological Science Report, USGS/BRD/BSR-01-1999.

Catallo, W. J., R.P. Gambrell, K. R. Reddy, J. H. Pardue, and J. Blankemeyer. 1999. Biogeochemical Processes, In: Ecotoxicology and Risk Assessment for Wetlands, ISBN:1-880611-16-3; SETAC Special Publication Series, SETAC Foundation for Environmental Education, Pensacola FL, pp. 27-69.

Junk, T. and W. J. Catallo. 1998. Environmental transformation products of 2,4,6-trinitrotoluene. Chem. Spec. Bioavail. 10(2):47-52.

1.10   Chapman, Russell, L.

Dr. Chapman is the Executive director at CCEER and a professor in the Dept. of Biological Sciences. He received his Ph.D. and M.S. from the University of California at Davis, his B.A. from Dartmouth College. His area of expertise is the molecular systematics of red algae.

Selected Publications:

Buchheim, M.A., Buchheim, J.A., and Chapman, R.L. 1997. Phylogeny of Chloromonas (Chlorophyceae): A study of ribosomal RNA gene sequences from the nucleus. J. Phycol. 33:286-293.

Meiers, S.T., Rootes, W.L., and Chapman, R.L. 1997. Phylogeny of genera in the Charales (Chlorophyta) inferred from morphological and molecular characters. Archiv fur Protistenkunde148:308-317.

Bailey, J.C. and Chapman, R.L. 1998. A phylogenetic study of the Corallinales (Rhodophyta) based on nuclear small-subunit rRNA gene sequences. J. Phycol. 34(4):692-705.

1.11   Current, Carol

Dr. Current is a physical oceanographer, with the New Orleans office of the Minerals Management Service. Environmental Studies Section. She received her B.A. in marine biology from San Francisco State University and a BS in electrical engineering from Texas A&M. MS and Ph.D degrees in physical oceanography followed at Texas A&M, where her dissertation work was part of the MMS-supported LATEX project. She continued her physical studies as an assistant professor-research in the Coastal Studies Institute of LSU. Her expertise includes implementation and testing of numerical models, parameter estimation, data analysis and dynamical interpretation, and model/data comparison in both deep and coastal waters.

Selected Publications:

Current, C.L., 1996: Spectral model simulation of wind driven subinertial circulation on the inner Texas-Louisiana shelf. Ph.D. thesis, Texas A&M University, 144 pp.

Current, C.L., 1993: Empirical vertical structure of density anomaly in the Gulf of Mexico. M.S. thesis, Texas A&M University, 143 pp.

Current, C. L., and R. O. Reid, 1998: Model simulation of wind-driven circulation on the inner Texas-Louisiana shelf: a comparison with 32 months of current and water level data. J. Geophys. Res., in review.

Current, C.L., and R. O. Reid, 1996: Wind driven, frictional flow on the inner Texas-Louisiana continental shelf: results of model/data comparison. EOS 76:39 (Abstr.).

Current, C. L., and W. J. Wiseman Jr. 2000. Dynamic height and seawater transport across the Louisiana-Texas shelf break. OCS Study MMS 2000-045. U. S. Dept. of the Interior, Minerals Management Service, Gulf of Mexico OCS Region, New Orleans, LA. 46 pp.

1.12   Dagg, Mike

Dr. Dagg is executive director the Louisiana Universities Marine Consortium and an adjunct professor of oceanography at LSU. He obtained his undergraduate degree at Mt. Allison University in New Brunswick Canada, a master's in marine biology at the University of Victoria, and a Ph.D in oceanography at the University of Washington. Dr. Dagg is a noted expert in oceanic zooplankton processes in an ecosystem context in a variety of systems including, high latitude boreal and Antarctic, and the Gulf of Mexico Mississippi River plume and Florida Bay.

Selected Publications:

Lohrenz, S.E., G.L. Fahnenstiel, D.G. Redalje, G.A. Lang, X. Chen and M.J. Dagg. 1997. Variations in primary production of northern Gulf of Mexico continental shelf waters linked to nutrient inputs from the Mississippi River. Mar. Ecol. Prog. Ser. 155: 45-54.

Dagg, M.J., B.W. Frost and J.A. Newton. 1998. Diel vertical migration and feeding in adult female Calanus pacificus, Metridia lucens and Pseudocalanus sp. during a spring bloom in Dabob Bay, a fjord in Washington USA. J. Mar. Systems 15: 503-509.

Lohrenz, S.E., G.L. Fahnenstiel, D.G. Redalje, G.A. Lang, M.J. Dagg, T.E. Whitledge and Q. Dortch. 1999. Nutrients, irradiance, and mixing as factors regulating primary production in coastal waters impacted by the Mississippi River plume. Cont. Shelf Res. 19: 1113-1141.

Dagg, M.J. 2000. Biological effects of Mississippi River nitrogen on the northern Gulf of Mexico - A review. J. Mar. Systems (in revision)

1.13   Deseran, Forrest A.

Dr. Deseran is a professor in the LSU Dept. of Sociology. He received his Ph.D. from Colorado State. His area of expertise is rural labor sociology.

Selected Publications:

Ten Eyck and Deseran. "Oysters in a Chiastic Sea: The Construction of a Local Social Issue," Louisiana Population Data Center Working Papers Series, 1997.

Deseran, F.A. Louisiana Shrimp Fishermen and Local Economies: Preliminary Survey Findings, Louisiana Sea Grant College Program, 1997.

Keithly, Diane and F. A. Deseran. 1995. "Households, Local Labor Markets, and Youth Labor Force Participation" Youth and Society 26:463-492.

Deseran, F. A. and D. Keithly. 1994. "Teenagers in the U.S. Labor Force: Local Labor Markets, Race, and Family" Rural Sociology 59:668-692.

1.14   Dinnell, Scott

Dr. Dinnell worked on a CMI project while an assistant professor in Marine Sciences at the University of Southern Mississippi. He received his Ph.D. from LSU. His interests include coastal physical dynamics.

1.15   Dismukes, David E.

David E. Dismukes is an assistant Professor at the Center for Energy Studies, Louisiana State
University. He received his B.A. from the University of West Florida in Pensacola, Florida, and his M.S. and Ph.D. degrees (economics) from the Florida State University, Tallahassee, Florida. His primary research interests are related to policy issues in regulated and energy industries. He is currently directing CES' research effort on electric utility restructuring and is serving as a policy advisor to the Louisiana Public Service Commission staff.

1.16   Dokken, Quenton R.

Dr. Dokken is the associate Director of the Center for Coastal Studies at TexasA&M University at Corpus Christi, Texas. He obtained his Ph.D. from Texas A&M, M.S. from Corpus Christi State University and B.S. from Texas A&I Professional Experience. He also serves as Executive Director, Gulf of Mexico Foundation. His expertise includes the ecology of reefs and artificial structures.

1.17   Donato, Katherine M.

Dr. Donato is an associate professor and director of graduate studies for the Dept, of Sociology at LSU. She received her Ph.D. from the State University of New York at Stony Brook. Her area of interest includes: Research interests lie in the areas of stratification and demography, and include international migration, immigration policy, and labor force activity and poverty of minority men and women in the United States.

Selected Publications:

Donato, Katharine M. 1998 "U.S. Policy on Illegal Immigration: A Thirty Year Retrospective." Forthcoming in David W. Haines and Karen E. Rosenblum (eds.), Illegal Immigration in America: A Reference Handbook. Greenwood Press.

Donato, Katharine M. and Deann Gauthier 1998 "Labor Prospects in Poverty Families: Puerto Ricans in New York and the United States." Forthcoming in Luis Falcon (ed.), Recasting Puerto Rican Poverty. Philadelphia, PA: Temple University Press.

Donato, Katharine M. and Shawn M. Kanaiaupuni 1998 "Women's Status and Demographic Change: Mexican Migration to the United States." Forthcoming in Brígida García and Karen Mason (eds.), Women, Poverty, and Demographic Change. Geneva: IUSSP.

1.18   Fleeger, John

Dr. John Fleeger is director of the Biology Program at LSU, having served as chair of Zoology and Physiology prior to departmental reorganization. Dr. Fleeger came to LSU after receiving a PhD in Zoology at the University of South Carolina, where he began studying meiofauna, especially harpacticoid copepods. His studies of meiofauna range from the species to the ecosystem level and cover a broad range of topics both basic and applied. Of special relevance to oil and gas studies, Dr. Fleeger's lab has been highly successful in maintaining experimental cultures and conducting rigorous experimental studies of contaminant effects.

Selected Publications:

Lotufo G. R. and J. W. Fleeger. 1997. Effects of sediment-associated phenanthrene on survival, development and reproduction of two species of meiobenthic copepods. Mar. Ecol. Prog. Ser. 151: 91-102.

1.19   Foltz, David

Dr. Folz is a professor in the department of Biological Sciences at LSU. He received his PhD from the University of Michigan and came to LSU following a postdoctoral fellowship at the University of Rochester and serving as a research associate at Dalhousie University. His research interest focus upon molecular evolution and populations of marine invertebrates. Most of his research has examined natural genetic variation. His participation in the CMI program applies the techniques of molecular genetics to the study of population-level changes due to oil and gas operations.

Selected Publications:

Hrincevich, A. W. and D. W. Foltz. 1996. Mitochondrial DNA sequence variation in a sea star (Leptasterias spp.) species complex. Molecular Phylogenetics and Evolution 6:408-415.

Foltz, D.W., J.P. Breaux, E.L. Campagnaro, S.W. Herke, A.E. Himel, A.W. Hrincevich, J.W. Tamplin and W.B. Stickle. 1996. Limited morphological differences between genetically identified cryptic species within the Leptasterias hexactis complex (Echinodermata: Asteroidea). Canadian Journal of Zoology 74:1275-1283.

Foltz, D. W., W. B. Stickle, E. L. Campagnaro and A. E. Himel. 1996. Mitochondrial DNA polymorphisms reveal additional genetic heterogeneity within the Leptasterias hexactis (Echinodermata: Asteroidea) species complex. Marine Biology 125:569-578.

1.20   Gauthreaux, Sidney A.

Dr. Gauthreaux is a professor of Biology at Clemson University, having received his M.S. and Ph.D. B.S., from LSU. His research interests include laboratory and field studies of bird migration, orientation and navigation.

Selected Publications:

Gauthreaux, S.A. 1992. The use of weather radar to monitor long-term patterns of trans-Gulf migration in spring. In: J.M. Hagan and D.W. Johnston (eds.) Ecology and conservation of neotropical migrant landbirds. Pp. 96-100. Smithsonian Institution Press, Washington, DC.

Moore, F.R., S.A. Gauthreaux, P. Kerlinger, and T.R. Simons. 1995. Habitat requirements during migration: Important link in conservation. Pp. 121-144 in Ecology and Management of Neotropical Migratory Birds: A Synthesis and Review of Critical Issues. (T.E. Martin and D.M Finch, eds.). Oxford University Press, NY.

Gauthreaux, S.A. 1996. Bird migration: Methodologies and major research trajectories (1945-1995). Condor 98(2):442-453.

Gauthreaux, S.A. and C.G. Belser. 1998. Displays of bird movements on the WSR-88D: Patterns and quantifications. Weather and Forecasting. July 1998.

1.21   Grambling, Robert B.

Dr. Grambling is a professor of sociology and anthropology at the University of Louisiana Lafayette. He received his Ph.D. from Florida State. His area of interest includes environmental sociology and social impact.

1.22   Guinasso, Norman L. Jr.

Dr. Guinasso is Deputy Director, Geochemical and Environmental Research Group, College of Geosciences and , Texas A&M University. He received his Ph.D. and M.S. from Texas A&M, B.A. from San Jose State College, also studyingh at the Universitaet Heidelberg. His area of expertise is Physical Oceanography, Marine Geochemistry, and Sedimentology.

Selected Publications:

Lewis, J. M., W. J. Martin, and N. L. Guinasso, Jr. 1997. Bowen Ratio estimates in return flow over the Gulf of Mexico. J. Geophys. Res 102(C5), 10535-10544.

MacDonald, I. R., J. R. Reilly, Jr., S. E. Best, R. Venkataramaiah, N. L. Guinasso, Jr. and Amos, 1996. Remote sensing inventory of active oil seeps and chemosynthetic communities in the Northern Gulf of Mexico. in D. Schumacher and M. A. Abrams, eds. Hydrocarbon Migration and its near-surface Expression, AAPG Memoir 66, 27-37.

DiMarco, S.F., F.J. Kelly, Jun Zhang, and N.L.Guinasso, Jr. 1995. Directional wave spectra on the Louisiana-Texas shelf during Hurricane Andrew. J. Coastal Res. SI 21, 217-233.

1.23   Hester, Mark W.

Dr. Hester is an associate professor in the Department of Biological Sciences at Southeastern Louisiana University, having begun work there in 1995 upon completion of his Ph.D. at LSU. He had previously earned a MS at LSU and a MS at Indiana University. His research interests include restoration ecology with emphasis on the use of vegetation to restore degraded wetland habitats and reduce coastal erosion ; plant stress ecophysiology of vegetation impacted by salinity, flooding and oil stress; plant ecology with emphasis on factors controlling the zonation and distribution of wetland vegetation; adaptations and responses of plants to natural and anthropogenic environmental stress; development of stress-specific indicators in wetland plants and selection techniques to identify superior stress-tolerant wetland vegetation; clonal plant ecophysiology; mechanisms of stress reduction in clonal plants.

Selected Publications:

DesRoches, D. J., G. P. Shaffer, M. W. Hester, and S. Miller. Submitted. A mesocosm approach to determine the suitability of processed drill cuttings for wetland restoration and creation. Ecological Engineering.

Dowty, R. A., G. P. Shaffer, M. W. Hester, G. W. Childers, F. M. Campo, and M. C. Greene. Submitted. Phytoremediation of small-scale oil spills in fresh marsh environments: a mesocosm simulation. Marine Environmental Research.

Hester, M. W., I. A. Mendelssohn. 1999. Long-term recovery of a Louisiana brackish marsh plant community from oil-spill impact: vegetation response and mitigating effects of marsh surface elevation. Marine Environmental Research 49: 1-22.

Pezeshki, R., M. W. Hester, Q. Lin, and J. A. Nyman. 1999. The effects of oil spill and clean-up on dominant US Gulf Coast marsh macrophytes: a review. Environmental Pollution 108: 1-11.

1.24   Hsu, Shiih-Ang

Dr. Hsu is a professor of Oceanography and Coastal Sciences and a researcher in the Coastal Studies Institute of LSU. He received both a Ph.D. and M.S. from the University of Texas and undergraduate training at the National University of Taiwan. His area of interest is coastal meteorology

Hsu. S. A. 1995. Measurements of SO_2 Concentration and Atmospheric Structure in Delta and Breton Wildlife Refuges. OCS Study MMS 95-0019. U.S. Dept. of the Interior, Minerals Management Service, Gulf of Mexico OCS Region, New Orleans, LA 74 pp.

Hsu, S. A. 1992.An overwater stability criterion for the offshore and coastal dispersion model. Boundary-Layer Meteorology, 60(4):397402

Hsu, S. A. 1989.A verification of analytical formula for estimating the height of the stable internal boundary layer. Boundary-Layer Meteorology, 48:197-201

Hsu, S. A. 1989. The relationship between the Monin-Obukhov stability parameter and the bulk Richardson number at sea. Journal of Geophysical Research (Oceans), 94, C6, 8053-8054.

1.25   Iledare, Omowumi O.

Dr. Illedare is an assistant professor/research, LSU Center for Energy Studies. He obtained his Ph.D. at West Virginia University, M.S. at the University of Pittsburgh, and B.S. at University of Ibadan, Nigeria. His research interests include: Oil and gas economics and policy analysis; Energy and the environment; and Energy supply modeling.

Selected Publications:

Iledare, O.O., A.G. Pulsipher A.G., D.F. Dismukes, and D.Mesyanzhinov. 1997. "Oil spills, workplace safety and firm size: evidence from the U.S. Gulf of Mexico OCS." The Energy Journal, 18 (4):73-89

Iledare, O.O. and A.G. Pulsipher. 1997. "The modeling of petroleum exploration and extraction process for policy analysis: a case study of Louisiana onshore Region." Pacific and Asian Journal of Energy,7 (1):21-38.

Iledare, O.O., A.G. Pulsipher, and R.H. Baumann. 1995. "Effects of an increasing role for, independents on petroleum resource development on the Gulf of Mexico OCS." The Energy Journal 16 (2):59-76.

1.26   Inoue, Masamichi

Dr. Inoue received his B.E. in naval architecture at Tokai University of Japan in 1973 and a M.S. in Ocean Engineering at University of Rhode Island in 1975. At Texas A&M University he obtained a M.E. in civil engineering in 1977 and a Ph.D. in Oceanography in 1982. Prior to coming to the Coastal Studies Institute at LSU, he held postdoctoral positions with the Mesoscale Air-Sea Interaction Group at Florida State University and the Australian Institute of Marine Science.

Selected Publications:

Inoue, M. and G.R. Bigg 1995. Trends in winds and sea-level pressure in the tropical Pacific Ocean for the period 1950-1979. International Journal of Climatology. 15:35-52.

Inoue, M., and S. E. Welsh. 1993. Modeling seasonal variability in the wind-driven upper-layer circulation in the Indo-Pacific region. Journal of Physical Oceanography 23:411-1436.

Bigg, G. R., and M. Inoue. 1992. Rossby waves and El Nino during 1935-46. Quarterly Journal of Royal Meteorological Society, 118, 125-152.

Inoue, M., J. J. O'Brien, W. B. White and S. E. Pazan,. 1987. Interannual variability in the tropical Pacific prior to the onset of the 1982/83 ENSO event. Journal of Geophysical Research, 92, 11, 671-11, 679.

1.27   Justic, Dubravko

Dr. Justic is an associate Professor in the LSU Department of Oceanography & Coastal Sciences/Coastal Ecology Institute. He received his Ph.D., M.S., and B.S. from the University of Zagreb. His research interests include: Ecosystem modeling, Marine coastal eutrophication and hypoxia, and Impacts of climate change on coastal ecosystems

Selected Publications:

Justic, D., Rabalais, N. N., Turner, R. 1999. Future perspectives for hypoxia in the northern Gulf of Mexico. In: Effects of Hypoxia on Living Resources, with Emphasis on the Northern Gulf of Mexico, (Rabalais, N. N. & Turner, R. E., eds.), AGU, Coastal and Estuarine Studies Series, in press.
Turner, R. E., Qureshi, N., Rabalais, N. N., Dortch, Q., Justic, D., Shaw, R., Cope, J. 1998. Fluctuating Silicate:Nitrate Ratios and Coastal Food Webs. Proc. Natl. Acad. Sci. USA,95: 13048-13051.
Justic, D., Rabalais, N. N., Turner, R. E. 1997. Impacts of climate change on net productivity of coastal waters: Implications for carbon budget and hypoxia. Climate Research, 8: 225-237.

1.28   Keithly, Walter R.

Dr. Keithly is an associate professor in the Center for Environmental Studies and the Coastal Fisheries Institute. He received his Ph.D. from the University of Georgia. His expertise lies in coastal resource economics.

Selected Publications:

Keithly, W. R. 1996. Economic Effects of Water Quality on Gulf of Mexico Region Oyster Production and Demand. Pages 303-313 In: Proceedings of the Gulf of Mexico Symposium on Improving Interactions Between Coastal Science and Policy. National Academy of Science Press, Washington, D.C. Peer reviewed.
Leard, R., B. Mahmoudi, H. Blanchet, H. Lazavski, K. Spiller, M. Buchanan, C. Dyer, and W. Keithly. 1995. The striped mullet fishery of the Gulf of Mexico: A regional management plan. Gulf States Marine Fisheries Commission.
Keithly, W. R. and K. J. Roberts. 1994. Central and South American shrimp and their role in the U.S. shrimp market. Proceedings of the 44th Gulf and Caribbean Fisheries Institute (peer review section).

1.29   LaRock, Paul A.

Dr. LaRock is a professor and former chair of Oceanography and Coastal Science at LSU. He received his Ph.D. and Rennasllyer. His area of expertise is marine microbial ecology.

Selected Publications:

Williams, L. A. and P. A. LaRock. 1986. The temporal occurrence of <u>Vibrio</u> species and <u>Aeromonas hydrophila</u> in estuarine sediments. <u>Appl. Environ. Microbiol. 50</u>:1490-1495.

LaRock, P. A., and T. Johengen. 1993. Quantifying nutrient removal processes within a constructed wetland designed to treat urban stormwater runoff. <u>Ecological Engineering</u>, 2:347-366.

LaRock, P. A. and J. H. Hyun. 1993. Bacterial growth rates measured by pulse labeling. In; Kemp, Sherr, Sherr and Cole, eds., <u>Current</u> <u>Methods</u> <u>in</u> <u>Microbial</u> <u>Ecology</u>, pp. 537- 546.

Koh, E. G. L., J. H. Hyun and P. A. LaRock. 1994. Pertinence of indicator organisms and sampling variables to Vibria concentrations. <u>Appl. Environ Microbiol.</u>, 60:3897-3900.

1.30   Laska, Shirley

Dr. Laska is a professor of sociology and Vice Chancellor for Research at the University of New Orleans. She received her Ph.D. from Tulane. Her interests include geographically proximal effects of coastal oil and gas development.

1.31   Lindau, Charles W.

Dr. Lindau is a Professor in the LSU Dept. of Oceanography and Coastal Sciences. He received his Ph.D. from Texas A&M University. His area of expertise includes soil chemistry especially nitrogen transformations in flooded soils and sediments, stable isotopic tracer techniques, measurements of greenhouse gases from flooded systems and environmental pollution and oil spill remediation.

1.32   Means, Jay C.

Dr. Means is the chair of the Department of Toxicology at the University of Western Michigan. Previously, he was a professor in the LSU Department of Veterinary Physiology, Pharmacology, and Toxicology. He received his Ph.D. from the University of Illinois. His interests include: Environmental chemistry of trace organics, trace metals and organometallics in sediment-water systems; analytical biochemistry and toxicology; organic geochemistry; chemical carcinogenesis; genetic toxicology; aquatic toxicology.

Selected Publications:

Law, J.M., D.J. McMillin, D.H. Swenson and J.C. Means. 1996. Quantification of DNA Adducts at Femtomole Levels in Fish Exposed to Alkylating Agents In. D.Bengtson and D. Herschel, eds. Environmental Toxicology and Risk Assessment, pp 117-137, ASTM STP 1306, West Conshohocken, PA.

Means, J.C. and McMillin, D.J. 1997. Evaluation of the bioconcentration potential of genotoxic contaminants in sediments using co-solvent mobilization. In. J.J Dwyer, T.R. Doane, and M.L. Hinman Eds. Environmental Toxicology and Risk Assessment,6th Volume, ASTM, Conshohocken, PA. pp 456-473.

Means, J.C. and A.E. McElroy. 1997. Bioaccumulation of tetra- and hexachlorobiphenyl by Yoldia limatula and Nepthys incisa from bedded sediments: Effects of Sediment and Animal Related Parameters. J. Env. Chem. Toxicol. 16:1277-1286.

1.33   Mendelssohn, Irving A.

Dr. Mendelsshon is a professor in the Dept. of Oceanography and Coastal Sciences and the Wetland Biogeochemistry Institute. He obtained his Ph.D. from North Carolina State University. His area of expertise includes physiological stress of coastal plants and coastal phytoremediation.

Selected Publications:

Mendelssohn, I. A. and K. L. McKee. 1987. Root metabolic response of Spartina alterniflora to hypoxia. ill "Plant Life in Aquatic and Amphibious Habitats" (R.M.M. Crawford, ed.); British Ecological Society Special Symposium. Special Publication No.5., pp.239-253.

Mendelssohn, I. A. and D. M. Burdick. 1988. The relationship of soil parameters and root metabolism to primary production in periodically inundated soils. Proceedings of the International Symposium on Ecology and Management of Wetlands, Charleston, S.C.

Mendelssohn, I. A., M. W. Hester, C. Sasser, and M. Fischel. 1990. The effect of a Louisiana crude oil discharge from a pipeline break on the vegetation of a southwest Louisiana brackish marsh. Oil and Chemical Pollution 7:1-15.

1.34   Mesyanzhinov, Dmitry

Dr. Mesyanzhinov is a full-time research associate in the LSU Center for Energy Studies. He received his Ph.D. from LSU and his B.A. from Moscow University. His area of expertise is economic geography, regional economics, statistical modeling, and computer cartography. He also has special technical expertise in the collection, management, and analysis of energy and socioeconomic data.

1.35   Murray, Stephen P.

Dr. Murray is a program director with the Office of Naval Research having retired from LSU as a professor in Oceanography and Coastal Sciences/Coastal Studies Institute. His area of expertise includes current systems in ocean straits.

Selected Publications:

Murray, S. T. and W. Johns, Direct Observations of Seasonal Exchange Through the Bab el Mandab Strait, Geophysical Research Letters, v.24, n. 21, pp. 2557-2560, November 1, 1997.

Arief, D. and S. P. Murray, Low Frequency Fluctuations in the Indonesian Throughflow through Lombok Strait, J. Geophysical Research, v.101, NOC 5, 12455-12464, 1996.

Murray, S. P., N. D. Walker and C. Adams: Impacts of Winter Storms on Sediment Transport Work in the Terrebonne Bay Marsh Complex. Coastal Zone 93, American Society Civil Engineers, New Orleans, 15 pages, 1993.

1.36   Overton, Edward B.

Dr. Overton is a professor and former director in the LSU Institute of Environmental Studies. He received his BS, and his Ph.D. in Chemistry at the University of Alabama. He is a noted expert in the evaluation of data from chemical spill incidents and subsequent recommendations for remediation. He has developed accurate and sophisticated field deployable analytical instrumentation to detect and identify toxic volatile chemicals

Selected Publication:

Overton, E. B. and Laseter, J. L., "Distribution of Aromatic Hydrocarbons in Sediments from Selected Atlantic. Gulf of Mexico. and Pacific Outer Continental Shelf Areas." Petroleum in the Marine Environment Advanced in Chemistry Series #185, 327-341 (1982).

Overton, E. B., C. F. Steele, S. B. Nauman, T. H. McKinney, and D. Kummerlowe, "Development of a Generally Applicable Field Usable Analytical Device for Hazardous Chemical Incidents", Proceedings of the HazMat 85 West Hazardous Materials Management Conference, Long Beach, CA, December 1985.

Overton, E. B., Schurtz, M. H., St. Pe', K. M. and Byrne, C., "Distribution of Trace Organics. Heavy Metals and Conventional Pollutants in Lake Pontchartrain Louisiana", in Marine and Estuarine Chemistry, Advances in Chemistry Series 305,247-270 (1985).

1.37   Penland, Patrick Shea

Dr. Penland is now the Braunstein Professor of Petroleum Geology in the Department of Geology and Geophysics at the University of New Orleans. He received his undergraduate education at the University of Jacksonville and MS and Ph.D. in Geography from LSU.   Dr. Shea Penland has more than 20 years of experience investigating the geology, geomorphology, and shoreline processes of the Gulf of Mexico, Alaska, U.S. Pacific and Atlantic coasts, Great Lakes; Canada, and the North Sea.

Selected Publications:

Williams, S. J., Penland, S., and Sallenger, A. H., Jr. 1992. Atlas of shoreline changes in Louisiana From 1985 to 1989. U.S. Geological Survey, Miscellaneous Investigations Series I1250A, 103 p.

Penland, S., Williams, S. J. Davis, D. W., Sallenger, A. H., Jr., and Groat, C. G. 1992. Barrier island erosion and wetland loss in Louisiana in Atlas of shoreline changes in Louisiana From 1985 to 1989. U.S. Geological Survey, Miscellaneous Investigations Series I-1250A, p.2-7.

McBride, R. A., Penland, S., Hiland, M. W., Williams, S. J., Westphal, K. A., Jaffe, B. E., and Sallenger, A. H., Jr. 1992. Analysis of barrier shoreline change in Louisiana from 1853 to 1989 in Atlas of shoreline changes in Louisiana from 1985 to 1989. U.S. Geological Survey, Miscellaneous Investigations Series I-1250A, p. 36-97.

1.38   Porrier, Ralph, J.

Dr. Porrier is past Director of the LSU Institute for Environmental Studies and Director of the Aquatic/Industrial Toxicology Laboratory. He received his Ph.D. and M.S. from LSU, B.S. from Nicholls State University. His areas of interest include: Fate and effect of carcinogens in fresh water and marine environments; Detoxification of contaminated soils and sediments by microorganisms; Wastewater treatment in the seafood industry Genetic engineering of marine microorganisms.

Selected Publications:

P.S. Razi, A. Raman and R. Portier 1997 Studies on mechanical properties of wood polymer composites. 1997. J. Composite Materials, Vol 31, No. 23, pp 2391-2401
R.J. Portier, D.L. Sattler, D.G. Hoover, T.M. Davis and S.E. Williams.1998 "Recovery and microbial remediation of organic wood preservatives in at a former wood treating plant" Remediation Vol 8,No. 4, pp 95-105.

1.39   Pulsipher, Allan G.

Allan G. Pulsipher is the Executive Director and Marathon Oil Company Professor of Energy Policy in the Center for Energy Studies and a Professor in Institute for Environmental Studies at LSU. He has a B.A. from the University of Colorado and a Ph.D. from Tulane University, both in economics. He currently is working on issues created by the changing oil and gas industry, especially those affecting the offshore part of the industry. He retains an active interest in policy issues related to the storage and disposal of high-level nuclear waste and the restructuring of the electricity industry-especially as it affects the Tennessee Valley Authority.

Selected Publications:

The Competitiveness of Louisiana's Petroleum Refining Industry, Center for Energy Studies, Louisiana State University, February 1993, pp. 53. with R. H. Baumann.
Assessing the Louisiana Natural Gas Distribution Industry in Residential and Commercial Markets, Center for Energy Studies, Louisiana State University, March 1993, pp. 39. with R. H. Baumann, W. O. Iledare, and D. Mesyanzhinov.
"Will Compensation Produce a Disposal Site?" Forum for Applied Research and Public Policy, Vol; 8; No.1, Spring 1993 pp. 108-114. Synopsis and discussion also printed in Energy Information Digest, No.98, April 1993, p.6.
"Anachronisms in Nuclear Waste Policy: The Case of the Integral MRS," Resources for the Future, Washington, DC, February 17, 1993.
"A De Facto Repository for the U.S.?" Energy Policy, forthcoming, 1993.

1.40   Rabalais, Nancy N.

Dr. Rabalais is a professor at LUMCON and holds an adjunct position in the LSU department of Oceanography and Coastal Sciences. She received her Ph.D. from the

University of Texas. Her interests include ecological impacts in coastal environments and coastal hypoxia.

Selected Publications:

Boesch, D. F. and N. N. Rabalais (eds.). 1987. Long-Term Environmental Effects of Offshore Oil and Gas Development. Elsevier Applied Science Publishers, London, 696 p.

Rabalais, N. N. and D. F. Boesch. 1987. Dominant features and processes of continental shelf Environments of the United States. Pages 71-147 in D. F. Boesch and N. N. Rabalais (eds.), Long-Term Environmental Effects of Offshore Oil and Gas Development. Elsevier Applied Science Publishers, London, 696 p.

Rabalais, N. N., R. E. Turner, W. J. Wiseman, Jr. and D. F. Boesch. 1991. A brief summary of hypoxia on the northern Gulf of Mexico continental shelf: 1985-1988. Pages 35-47 in R.V. Tyson and T.H. Pearson (eds.) Modern and Ancient Continental Shelf Anoxia, Geological Society Special Publication No.58, The Geological Society, London, 470 p.

Rabalais, N. N. 1990. Biological communities of the south Texas continental shelf. Amer. Zool. 30(1):77-87.

Rabalais, N. N. and J. N. Cameron. 1985. Physiological and morphological adaptations of adult *Uca subcylindrica* to semi-arid environments. Biol. Bull. 168:135-146.

1.41   Remsen, James V. Jr.

Dr. Remsen is Curator and Adjunct Professor in the Museum of Natural Science and Department of Biological Sciences. He received his Ph.D. from the University of California at Berkeley. His interests include the ecology, evolution, and zoogeography of Neotropical birds, particularly those of the Andes and the Amazon Basin.

Selected Publications:

Remsen, J. V., Jr., S. W. Cardiff, and D. L. Dittmann. 1996. Timing of migration and status of vireos (Vireorndae) in Louisiana. J. Field Ornithology 67:119-140.

Remsen, J. V., Jr., and D. A. Good. 1996. Misuse of data from mist-net captures to measure relative abundance in bird populations. Auk 113: 381-398.

Remsen, J. V., Jr. 1995. The importance of continued collecting of specimens to ornithology and bird conservation. Bird Conservation International 5:145-180.

Remsen, J. V., Jr., and W. S. Graves. 1995. Distribution patterns and zoogeography of *Atlapetes* brush-finches (Emberizinae) of the Andes. Auk 112: 210-224.

1.42   Roberts, Harry

Dr. Roberts is director of the Coastal Studies Institute and professor of Oceanography and Coastal Sciences. He received his Ph.D. and M.S. from LSU and his B.S. from Marshall University. His area of expertise includes slope geomorphology.

Selected Publications:

Roberts, H. H., O. K. Huh, S. A. Hsu, L. J. Rouse, Jr. and D. Rickman. 1989. Winter storm impact on the Chenier Plain coast of southwestern Louisiana: Transactions Gulf Coast Geological Societies, 39:512-522.

Roberts, H. H., O. K. Huh, S. A. Hsu, L. J. Rouse, Jr. and D. Rickerman. 1987. Impact of cold-front passages on geomorphic evolution and sediment dynarnics of the complex Louisiana coast: Coastal Sediments '87 (ASCE), New Orleans, Louisiana, 1950-1963.

Roberts, H. H., R. D. Adams, and R. H. W. Cunnigham. 1980. Evolution of the sand~rninant subaerial phase, Atchafalaya Delta, Louisiana: American Association of Petroleum Geologists Bull., 64:264-279.

1.43   Rouse, Larry L. Jr

Dr. Rouse is the director of the phase II CMI program and an associate professor in the LSU department of Oceanography and Coastal Sciences/Coastal Studies Institute. He received his Ph.D. from LSU. His interests include remote sensing physical oceanography.

Selected Publications:

Huh, O.K., C.C. Moeller, W.P.Menzel, L.J. Rouse, Jr., and H.H. Roberts, 1996, Remote sensing of turbid coastal and estuarine waters: a method of multispectral water-type analysis. Journal of Coastal Research 12(4):984-995.

Walker, N.D., O.K. Huh, L.J. Rouse, and S.P. Murray, 1996, Evolution and structure of a coastal squirt off the Mississippi River Delta: northern Gulf of Mexico. Journal of Geophysical Research 101(C9):20,643-20,655.

Day, Jr., J.W. Madden, R.R. Twilley, R.F. Shaw, B.R. McKee, M.J. Dagg, D.L. Childers, R.C. Raynie, and L.J. Rouse, 1995, The influence of Atchafalaya River discharge on Fourleague Bay, Louisiana (USA). Changes in Fluxes in Estuaries, ECSA22/ERF Sumpo sium, pp. 151-160.

1.44   Sen Gupta, Barun

Dr. Sen Gupta is a professor of Geology and Geophysics at LSU. He received his Ph. D., from the Indian Institute of Technology, Kharagpur, India. His research interests include the geological record and modern distribution of benthic foraminifera, especially Quaternary water masses of the Caribbean Sea and Gulf of Mexico.

Selected Publications:

Denne, R. A., and B. K. Sen Gupta. 1989. Effects of taphonomy and habitat on the record of benthic foraminifera in modern sediments. Palaios 4: 414-423.

Cassell, D. T., and B. K. Sen Gupta. 1989. Pliocene foraminifera and environments, Lim Basin of Costa Rica. Jour. Paleontology 63: 146-158.

Sen Gupta, B. K., R. F. Lee, and M. T. May. 1981. Upwelling and an unusual assemblage of benthic foraminifera on the northern Florida continental slope. Jour. Paleontology 55: 853-857.

1.45   Scott, Max

Dr. Scott is the LSU System radiation safety officer and holds an appointment as an associate professor in the Nuclear Science Center at LSU. After receiving his PhD from Perdue University he served in the radiation health field for Union Carbide and Gulf Oil Corporation. He joined LSU in 1985. His professional expertise includes radiation safety and NORMs, Naturally Occurring Radioactive Material, especially associated with oil and gas.

1.46   Shaw, Richard F.

Dr. Shaw is director of the LSU Coastal Fisheries Institute and professor of Oceanography and Coastal Sciences. He received his Ph.D. at the University of Maine at Orono and his undergraduate degree at Merrimack College. His interests include larval fish population dynamics and larval fish associations with artificial structures.

Selected Pulications:

Raynei, R. C. and R. F. Shaw. 1994. Ichthyoplankton abundance along a recruitment corridor from offshore spawning to estuarine nursery ground. *Estuar. Coastal Sbelf* Sci., 39: 421-449.
Lazzari, M. A., D. K. Stevenson and R. F. Shaw. 1993. Influence of tidal flow and vertical distribution on the abundance and retention of larval Atlantic herring *(Clupea harengus)* in a Maine estuary. Can. J. Fish. Aquat. Sci., 50:1879-1890.
Whitehurst, A. E., R. F. Shaw, D. L. Leffler, T. Farooqi and J. G. Ditty. (Submitted). Macrozooplankton biomass and composition - abundance and patchiness of ichthyoplankton from offshore waters of the Louisiana-Mississippi Barrier Islands: August-November 1986-1990. *Bull. Mar. Sci.*

1.47   Russell, Robert W.

Dr. Russell is an assistant professor/research in the special programs division of CCEER at LSU. He began CMI studies as a postdoc in the LSU Museum of Natural History. He received his Ph.D. from the University of California at Irvine.

1.48   Shihadeh, Edward S.

Dr. Shihadeh is a professor of sociology at LSU. He received his BS and MS at the University of Alberta and his PhD at Pennsylvania State University. His research interests include criminology, demography, and research methods,

Selected Publications:

Shihadeh, E.S. and G. Ousey. 1995. Metropolitan expansion and black social dislocations: The link between suburbanization and center-city crime. Social Forces 74:144-156.
Shihadeh, E.S. 1995. An Overview of the census net population undercount.
Godart:Documents to the People, 23.

Shihadeh, E.S. 1991. The prevalence of husband centered migration employmeny consequences for married mothers. Journal of Marriage and the Family 53:432-444.

1.49   Singelmann, Joachim

Dr. Singleman is a joint professor and former chairman in the LSU departments of Sociology and Rural Sociology. He received is undergraduate education at the University of Hamburg ands his master's and Ph.D in sociology at the University of Texas. He came to LSU from the Population Division of the United Nations. His research interests focus regionally on coastal resource issues and internationally on the impacts of German reunification.

Selected Publications:

Singelmann, Joachim. 1996. "Will Rural Areas Still Matter in the 21st Century? (or) Can Rural Sociology Remain Relevant?" Rural Sociology 61:143-158.

Singelmann, Joachim, and Dieter Urban. 1996. "Demokratieverstandnis zwischen Euphoric und Ernuchterung: Eine Thuringer Fallstudie, 1992-95" (Support for Liberal Democra~ from Euphoria to Reality: A Cave Study in Thuringia, 1992-95). Pp. 229-250 in M. Diewald and K.-U. Mayer (ed.), Zwiscbenbilai'z der Wiedervereinigung: Strukturwandel und Mobilitat. Opladen: Leske & Buderich.

Singelmann, Joachim, Yoshinori Kamo, Alan C. Acock, and Michael D. Grimes. 1996. "Dual-Earner Families and the Division of Household Labor: A Comparative Analysis of Six Industrial Societies."Acta Demographica 5:159-178.

Singelmann, Joachim. 1994. "Agricultural Transformation and Social Change in an East German County." Pp. 65-84 in D.A. Kideckel (ed.), E'L%t Europe~in Communities: The Struggle for balance in Turbuleot Times. Boulder, CO: Westview Press.

1.50   Stanley, David Robert

Dr. Stanley participated in CMI projects while a postdoctoral student at LSU. He received his Ph.D and M.S. from LSU and his undergraduate trailing at the University of Guelph. His area of interest includes hydroacoustic assessment of fish populations and fish assemblages of offshore structures.

Selected Publications:

Stanley, D.R., and C.A. Wilson. In press. Variation in the density and species composition of fishes associated with three petroleum platforms as measured with dual beam hydroacoustics. Proceedings 1997 AFS Acoustic Symposium, American Fisheries Society, Monterey CA. Fisheries Science.

Stanley, D.R., and C.A. Wilson. 1999. Spatial variation in fish density at three petroleum platforms as measured with dual-beam hydroacoustics in the northern Gulf of Mexico. Proceedings 1997 AFS Artificial Reef Symposium, American Fisheries Society, Monterey CA. Gulf Science.

Stanley, D.R., and C.A. Wilson. 1996. The use of hydroacoustics to determine abundance and size distribution of fishes associated with a petroleum platform. International Council on the Exploration of the Sea, Journal of Marine Science. 53:473-475.

1.51   Stickle, William B., Jr.

Dr Stickle is a professor in the LSU department of Biological Sciences. He received his Ph.D. from the University of Saskatchewan. His area of interest includes echinoderm physiological ecology and stress induced enzyme systems.

Selected Publications:

Roller, R. A. and W. B. Stickle. 1993. Salinity and Temperature Acclimation Effects on the Larval Tolerance, Physiology, and Early Development of *Lytechinus vafiegatus* (Lamarck) (Echinodermata: Echinoidea). Marine Biology (In press).

Stickle, W. B., S. Y. Wang, S. D. Rice, and J. W. Short. 1993. Effects of TBT exposure feeding rates, growth and limb loss of the juvenile blue crab, Callinectes sapidus. Marine Environmental Research (submitted).

Das, T. and W. B. Stickle. 1993. Sensitivity of the southern oyster drill, *Stfamonita haemastoma,* the blue crab, *Callinectes sapidus* and the lesser blue crab, *Callinectes similis,* to hypoxia and anoxia. Marine Ecology Progress Series (in press).

1.52   Stone, Gregory

Dr. Stone is a professor of Oceanography and Coastal Sciences and in the Coastal Studies Institute. He received hios Ph.D. from the University of Maryland, M.S. from The University of West Florida, and BSc. from the University of Ulster. His area of expertise includes the dynamics of coastal wave fields.

Selected Publications:

Stone, G.W., Grymes, J.M., Armbruster, C.A. and Huh, O.K. "Researchers Study Impact of Hurricane Opal on Florida Coast." Earth in Space, 9, 1, 7-9. 1996

Stone, G.W. and Stapor, F.W. "A Nearshore Sediment Transport Model of the Northeast Gulf of Mexico Coast, U.S.A. Journal of Coastal Research, 12. 3. 786-792, 1996

Chaney, P., and Stone, G.W. Soundside Erosion of A Nourished Beach and Implications for Winter Cold Front Forcing: West Ship Island, Mississippi. Journal of American Assoc. Shore and Beach Pres. Assoc. 64(1):27-33.

1.53   Tolbert, Charles M., II

Dr. Tolbert is now chairman of the Department of Sociology at Baylor University. While at LSU he was a professor in the Department of Sociology and Rural Sociology, serving as chair at the time of his departure. He received his undergraduate training at Baylor and received a Ph.D. in sociology from the University of Georgia. His areas of interest include labor market analysis.

Selected Publication:

Lyson, Thomas and Charles M. Tolbert. In Press. Small Manufacturing and Civic Welfare in U.S Nonmetropolitan Counties: A Regional Comparison. *Environment and Planning A*.

Killian, Molly S. and Charles M. Tolbert. 1993. Mapping Social and Economic Space: The Methodology of Defining Local Labor Markets. Pp. 69-79 in Singelmann, Joachim and F. A. Deseran (eds.), Inequality in Local Labor Markets, Boulder: Westview.

Coldough, Glenna and Charles M. Tolbert. 1993. Divisions of Labor and Inequality in High-Tech Centers. Pp. 143-63 in Singelmann, Joachim and F. A. Deseran (eds.), Inequality in Local Labor Markets, Boulder: Westview.

1.54   Tootle, Debora

Dr. Tootle is a sociologist with the Louisana Extension Service. She was previously an assitant research professor in the LSU Department of Rural Sociology and the Louisiana Population Data Center. She received her undergraduate training at LSU, earning a MS from Tulane and a Ph.D. from the University of Georgia.

Selected Publications:

Tootle, D.M. 1990. Nonmetro income growth sluggish. Rural Conditions and Trends 1:14-15.

Tootle, D.M. 1987. Labeling and social acceptance of the recovering alcoholic in the workplace. Journal of Drug Issues, summer 273-279.

Tootle, D.M. and S. Green. 1989. The effect of ethnic identity on support for farm worker unions. Rural Sociology 54:83-91.

1.55   Turner, Robert E.

Dr. Turner is professor of Oceanography and Coastal Science and Director of the Coastal Ecology Institute. He received his Ph.D. from the University of Georgia, M.S. from Drake University, and B.A. from Monmouth College. His area of interest includes: Biological oceanography, Conservation, Environmental management, and Fisheries ecology.

Selected Publications:

Turner, R. E. and M. E. Boyer. 1997. Mississippi River diversions, coastal wetland restoration/creation and an economy of scale. Ecological Engineering (in press).

Turner, R. E. 1997. Book Review: *Ecology and Management of Tidal Marshes: A Model from the Gulf of Mexico,* edited by C. L. Colts and Y-P Hsieh. Estuaries 20(1): (in press).

Turner, R. E. 1997. Wetland loss in the northern Gulf of Mexico: Multiple working hypotheses. Estuaries 20 (1): (in press).

1.56   Van Gent, Daniel

Mr. Van Gent is a research specialist in the LSU Nuclear Science Center and assistant radiation safety officer for the campus. He reveived a B.S. in environmental science from U.C. Davis, and a MS in nuclear science at LSU.

1.57   Wilson, Vincent L.

Dr. Wilson is a faculty member in the LSU Institute for Environmental Studies. He received his Ph.D. from Oregon State, M.S.from University of California at Davis, and B.S. from Sonoma State University. His research interests include: Toxicology of environmental pollutants and other genotoxic agents with emphasis on mechanisms in mutagenesis and carcinogenesis.

1.58   Walker, Nan Delene

Dr. Walker is an associate professor/research in the Coastal Studies Institute and Dept. of Oceanography and Coastal Sciences. She is associate Director for the Earth Scan Laboratory. She received her Ph.D. from the University of Cape Town, M.S. from LSU, and B.S. from Duke University. Her research interests include: Satellite oceanography, Ocean climatology, Ocean-atmosphere interactions, Coastal upwelling, Coastal and shelf circulation, and Physical-biological interactions,

Selected Publications:

Walker, N. D., Satellite Assessment of Mississippi River Plume Variability: Causes and Predictability, Remote Sensing of Environment, in press.
Walker, N. D., O. K. Huh, L. J. Rouse, and S. P. Murray, Evolution and Structure of a Coastal Squirt off the Mississippi River Delta: Northern Gulf of Mexico, Journal of Geophysical Research, in press.
Hitchcock. G. L., W. J. Wiseman, Jr., W. C. Boicourt, A.J. Mariano, N. Walker, T. Nelson, and E Ryan, Property fields in an effluent plume of the Mississippi River, Journal of Marine Systems, submitted.

1.59   Walsh, Maud

Dr. Walsh is a research scientist in the LSU Institute for Environmental Studies. She received her Ph.D, and M.S. from LSU, and B.A. from Bryn Mawr. He interests include: Geomicrobiology, Bioremediation, and Early life on Earth.

Selected Publications:

Walsh, M. M. and Lowe, D. R. 1999. Modes of accumulation of carbonaceous matter in the early Archean: a petrographic and geochemical study of the carbonaceous cherts of the Swaziland Supergroup, in Geological Society of America Special Paper 329, pp. 115-132.
Walsh, M. M. and Seckbach, J. 1999. The Versatility of Prokaryotes. In: J. Seckbach, (ed.), The Netherlands: Kluwer Academic Publishers, pp. 153-162.

Byerly, G. R., Kroner, A., Lowe, D. R., Todt, W., and Walsh, M. M. 1996. Prolonged magmatism and time constraints for sediment deposition in the early Archean Barberton greenstone belt; evidence from the Upper Onverwacht and Fig Tree groups. Precambrian Research 78: 125-138.

1.60   Wayne, Linda

Ms Wayne is a research scientist in the Special Projects Program of the LSU Center for Coastal and Energy Resources. She received her bachelor's in landscape architecture from Virginia Polytechnic Institute in 1983 and worked a commercial land planner until beginning graduate studies at LSU. She received her masters in landscape architecture in 1993. During her graduate study she worked as a research assistant and system coordinator.

Selected Publications:

Wayne, L.D., N. Froomer, P. Bottenberg, and J. Dahlin. 1997. Gulf-wide Information System (G-WIS) Data Specification Manual, Ver. 2.1 US Minerals Management Service. New Orleans, :a. 132. Pages.
Wayne, L.D., and J.D. Register. 1995. Management and Distribution of Geospatial Coastal data and Information. Coastal Zone 95. American Society of Civil Engineers NY, NY. Pp. 336-337.
Wayne, L.D. , M.R. Byrnes, and J.D. Hayden. 1994. An analytical model for classifying Land loss in Lousiana. Second Thematic Conference- Remote Sensing for Marine and Coastal Environments. Environmenta.l Reserarch Institute of Michigan ERIM, New Orleans, La. 1:679-685.

1.61   Dr. Susan Welsh

Dr. Welsh received her BA in Earth and Planetary Science at Johns Hopkins University in 1983 and her MS in oceanography at Florida State in 1986. She worked as a scientific programmer in the Dept. of Oceanography at Florida state until 1989 and then assumed similar duties in the Coastal Studies Institute at LSU. She was awarded a prestigious Regents graduate fellowship and completed her Ph.D. in geology and Geophysics in 1996. Integral to her graduate work was CMI-supported simulation of circulation in the Gulf of Mexico. Dr. M. Inoue served as her major advisor.

Selected Publications:

Welsh, S.E. and M. Inoue. 1997. A numerical model of the deep circulation in the Gulf of Mexico. Journal of Physical Oceanography. Submitted
Welsh, S.E. and M. Inoue. 1997. A numerical modeling of the upper-layer seasonal circulation in the Gulf of Mexico. Journal of Physical Oceanography. Submitted
Welsh, S.E. and M. Inoue. 1993. Modeling seasonal variability in the wind-driven upper-layer circulation in the Indo-Pacific region. Journal of Physical Oceanography. 23:1411-1436.
Sturges, W. and S.A. Welsh. 1990. On the wind-driven response of ocean surface IR signals. Journal of Physical Oceanography. 20:1842-1848

1.62   Wilson, Charles A. III

Dr. Wilson is in the Coastal Fisheries Institute at LSU and chairman of the Department of Oceanography and Coastal Sciences. He received his Ph.D. from the University of Alabama. His interests include artificial habitat construction, age, growth, and reproductive biology of fish and mariculture.

Selected Publications:

Wilson, C. A., D. Dunkelberger, N. C. Alon, and M. C. Rubino. 1990. Tidal pond culture in South Carolina; A sustainable alternative for shrimp mariculture. Aquaculture 1 6(4):54-61.

Rubino, M. C., N. C. Alon, C. A. Wilson, and J. M. Armstrong. 1990. Marron aquaculture research in the United States and the Caribbean. Aquaculture 1 6(3):27-43.

Render, J. H., and C. A. Wilson. (In Press). A description of reproductive biology of sheepshead in the Northern Gulf of Mexico. Trans. Am. Fish. Soc. selected Refereed Publications:

1.63   Winston, Gary W.

Dr. Winston is chair and professor of the Dept. of Toxicology at North Carolina State University. He previously served as chair of Biochemistry at LSU. He received is Ph.D. from the University of Nevada at Los Vegas. His interests include induced stress enzyme systems in marine organisms.

Selected Publications:

Livingstone, D. R., Martinez, P. G., Stegeman, J. J. and Winston, G.W. Beno[a]pyrene metabolism and aspects of oxygen radical generation in the common mussel *Mytilus edulis* L. Biochem. Soc. Transact., 16:779-780 (1988).

Jewell, C. S. E. and Winston, G. W. Oxyradical production by hepatopancreas microsomes from the red swamp crayfish, *Procambasus clarkil*, Aquat. Toxicol. 14: 27-46 (1989).

Jewell, C. S. E. and Winston, G. W. Characterization of the microsomal mixed-function oxygenase system of the hepatopancreas and green gland of the red swamp crayfish, *Procambasus clarkii.* Comp.Biochem. Physiol., 92B: 329-339 (1989).

1.64   Wiseman, William Joseph

Dr. Wiseman is currently with the Physical Oceanography Program at NSF, on leave from his position as professor in Oceanography and Coastal Sciences/Coastal Studies. He received his Ph.D. from The Johns Hopkins University. His research interests include: coastal and estuarine dynamics; interactions of physical processes with both biological and geological processes in coastal and estuarine environments.

Selected Publications:

Wiseman, Wm. J., Jr. and R. W. Garvine. 1995. Plumes and Coastal Currents near Large River Mouths. Estuaries. 18(3):509-517.

Wiseman, Wm. J., Jr. and F. J. Kelly. 1994. Salinity variability within the Louisiana Coastal Current during the 1982 flood season. Estuaries! 17(4):732-739.

Lee, J. M., Wm. J. Wiseman, Jr. and F. J. Kelly. 1990. Barotropic sub-tidal exchange between Calcasieu Lake and the Gulf of Mexico, Estuaries, 13(3): 258-264.

The Department of the Interior Mission

As the Nation's principal conservation agency, the Department of the Interior has responsibility for most of our nationally owned public lands and natural resources. This includes fostering sound use of our land and water resources; protecting our fish, wildlife, and biological diversity; preserving the environmental and cultural values of our national parks and historical places; and providing for the enjoyment of life through outdoor recreation. The Department assesses our energy and mineral resources and works to ensure that their development is in the best interests of all our people by encouraging stewardship and citizen participation in their care. The Department also has a major responsibility for American Indian reservation communities and for people who live in island territories under U.S. administration.

The Minerals Management Service Mission

As a bureau of the Department of the Interior, the Minerals Management Service's (MMS) primary responsibilities are to manage the mineral resources located on the Nation's Outer Continental Shelf (OCS), collect revenue from the Federal OCS and onshore Federal and Indian lands, and distribute those revenues.

Moreover, in working to meet its responsibilities, the **Offshore Minerals Management Program** administers the OCS competitive leasing program and oversees the safe and environmentally sound exploration and production of our Nation's offshore natural gas, oil and other mineral resources. The MMS **Minerals Revenue Management** meets its responsibilities by ensuring the efficient, timely and accurate collection and disbursement of revenue from mineral leasing and production due to Indian tribes and allottees, States and the U.S. Treasury.

The MMS strives to fulfill its responsibilities through the general guiding principles of: (1) being responsive to the public's concerns and interests by maintaining a dialogue with all potentially affected parties and (2) carrying out its programs with an emphasis on working to enhance the quality of life for all Americans by lending MMS assistance and expertise to economic development and environmental protection.